Lorraine Hansberry's

A Raisin in the Sun

Thirtieth Anniversary Edition
(Revised)

SAMUEL FRENCH

FOUNDED 1830

New York Hollywood London Toronto
SAMUELFRENCH.COM

Lorraine Hansberry's

A Raisin in
the Sun

Thirtieth Anniversary Edition
(Revised)

SAMUEL FRENCH

ABOUT LORRAINE HANSBERRY
and "A RAISIN IN THE SUN"

*"I am a writer. I suppose I think that the highest
gift that man has is art, and I am audacious enough
to think of myself as an artist — that there is both
joy and beauty and illumination and communion
between people to be achieved through the dissection of personality. That's what I want to do. I
want to reach a little closer to the world, which is to
say to people, and see if we can share some illuminations together about each other."*

— Lorraine Hansberry, *To Be Young, Gifted and Black*

(*continued on p. 157*)

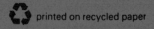

What happens to a dream deferred?
Does it dry up
Like a raisin in the sun?
Or fester like a sore —
And then run?
Does it stink like rotten meat?
Or crust and sugar over —
Like a syrupy sweet?

Maybe it just sags
Like a heavy load.

Or does it explode?
                    — Langston Hughes

To Mama:
in gratitude for the dream

A NOTE ABOUT THIS EDITION

This edition, like the 25th anniversary edition, restores to *A Raisin in the Sun* a number of scenes, lines and passages cut from the original production which Lorraine Hansberry later felt were important to the play. And it incorporates in the stage directions the fresh insights and discoveries of later productions that enhance the impact and import, humor, power, resonance of particular moments and the play overall.

"It is one of a handful of great American dramas...*A Raisin in the Sun* belongs in the inner circle, along with *Death of a Salesman, Long Day's Journey into Night,* and *The Glass Menagerie."* So wrote the Washington Post of the revelatory 25th anniversary Roundabout Theatre revival at the Kennedy Center in which the above elements were most effectively combined. The unprecedented resurgence of the work that continues with no end in sight (a dozen major revivals at this writing and an American Playhouse production of the unabridged play for television) occasions the new edition.

Produced in 1959, the play presaged the revolution in black and women's consciousness — and the revolutionary ferment in Africa — that exploded in the years following the playwright's death in 1965 to alter ineradicably the social fabric and consciousness of the nation. It did so in a manner and to an extent, as so many have commented lately, that few could have foreseen. For not only the excised material, but much else that passed unnoticed in the play at the time speaks to issues and concerns that are now inescapable: value systems of the black family; concepts of African American beauty, identity, hairstyle; class and generational conflicts; the relationships of husband and wife, black men and women; the (then yet unnamed) feminism of Beneatha; and, in the penultimate Beneatha/Asagai scene, the larger statement of the play — and the ongoing struggle it portends.

Not one of the cuts, it should be emphasized, was made to dilute or censor the play, but for reasons specific to the dynamics of that first mounting, and the exigencies and realities (both commercial and racial) of Broadway. The history of the play and of some of the cuts is discussed in my Foreword to the 1987 New American Library double-edition with *The Sign in Sidney Brustein's Window.*

Hansberry put many of these cuts (there were also good ones that honed and tightened the play) back in the Random House reading version, but she later felt that some others — the bedtime scene between Walter and Travis (eliminated on Broadway) and the Beneatha-Asagai scene (drastically cut) — should be restored at the first opportunity, and this was done in a 1966 edition. The one about Beneatha's hair was published for the first time in the 1984 acting edition.

Running time of the play (two ten-minute intermissions included) should now be about three hours. If that presents a serious problem for your theatre, those restorations have been bracketed which might, at least cost to the work, be sacrificed. Such cuts are not recommended, however, and, alternatively, you might consider presenting the play in two acts, with the break coming either after Act One or Act Two, Scene One; both have been tried and worked well.

Two other scenes are included here as an addendum. The first, with Mrs. Johnson, makes plain the realities and dangers that await the Youngers at final curtain and, above all, that Lena Younger is anything but the "conservative" voice of acceptance some have portrayed her as being. But the scene adds another character and seven or eight minutes to the play. For this reason it has not been used in the major revivals, though in several others it has worked to great —

and hilarious — effect. It is included here as background for actors and director, and as an option.

Published for the first time, the second scene makes tangible and visceral one of the many facts of ghetto life that impel the Youngers' move, and should put to rest for all time the notion that this is a "middleclass" family. At its full potential, the scene can be seen in the American Playhouse production. But without such exceptional acting in the roles of both Ruth *and Travis,* the scene can shatter, rather than enhance, audience involvement. It is not, therefore, a scene to be undertaken lightly.

A word about the stage directions. This acting edition combines the author's interpretive directions with the staging insights and contributions of two great directors and companies: Lloyd Richards' classic staging of that now legendary cast who first created the roles; and Harold Scott's, whose searching explorations of the text in successive revivals over many years — culminating in the inspired production that broke box office records at the Kennedy Center in 1986, toured other cities, and won ten NAACP Theatre Image Awards for Scott and the company — have given the full text, in my view, its most definitive realization to date. Because there have been, in effect, not one but *two* such seminal productions, I am listing below the collective creators of both.

Finally, a note about the American Playhouse production, which should be available on videocassette shortly. Unlike the drastically cut and largely one-dimensional 1961 movie version, which reflected little of the greatness of the original on-stage performances (pioneering a film as it may have been in its day), the television production reflects the full values of the play. Because of a happenstance in the shooting, it omits one key scene. But it is based on Scott's stage production, as brilliantly reconceived and reblocked cinematically by director Bill Duke with incisive variations

7

of his own—and with two exceptions (Danny Glover in a classic performance as Walter Lee and Helen Martin as Mrs. Johnson) it features the same cast. The scene will be restored on videocassette. It is thus an excellent version for study.

October 1988

Robert Nemiroff
Executor, the Estate of
Lorraine Hansberry

A RAISIN IN THE SUN by Lorraine Hansberry was first staged by Lloyd Richards; settings and lighting by Ralph Alswang; costumes by Virginia Volland; presented by Philip Rose and David J. Cogan at the Ethel Barrymore Theatre, N.Y.C., March 11, 1959, with the following cast:

CAST OF CHARACTERS
(*in order of appearance*)

RUTH YOUNGER	Ruby Dee
TRAVIS YOUNGER	Glynn Turman
WALTER LEE YOUNGER (Brother)	Sidney Poitier
BENEATHA YOUNGER	Diana Sands
LENA YOUNGER (Mama)	Claudia McNeil
JOSEPH ASAGAI	Ivan Dixon
GEORGE MURCHISON	Louis Gossett
BOBO	Lonne Elder 3rd
KARL LINDNER	John Fiedler
TWO MOVING MEN	Ed Hall, Douglas Turner Ward

The Twenty-fifth Anniversary Production was staged by Harold Scott; settings by Tom Cariello; lighting by Shirley Prendergast; costumes by Judy Dearing; sound by Rick

Menke and Philip Campanella; presented by the Roundabout Theatre Company, Inc. (Gene Feist/Todd Haimes)
and Robert Nemiroff at the Kennedy Center, Washington,
D.C., November 16, 1986, with the following cast:

RUTH YOUNGER .... Starletta DuPois
TRAVIS YOUNGER .... Kimble Joyner
WALTER LEE YOUNGER .... Delroy Lindo
BENEATHA YOUNGER .... Kim Yancey
LENA YOUNGER (MAMA) .... Esther Rolle
JOSEPH ASAGAI .... Lou Ferguson
GEORGE MURCHISON .... Joseph C. Phillips
BOBO .... Stephen Henderson
KARL LINDNER .... John Fiedler
MOVING MEN........ Ron O.J. Parson, Charles Watts

The action takes place in the Younger's apartment on
Chicago's Southside, in the early 1950's.

PRODUCTION NOTES

The Younger living room would be a comfortable and
well-ordered room, if it were not for a number of in-
destructible contradictions to this state of being. It's furnishings are typical and undistinguished and their
primary feature now is that they have clearly had to accommodate the living of too many people for too many
years—and they are tired. Still, we can see, at some
time, a time probably no longer remembered by the
family (except perhaps for Mama), the furnishings of
this room were actually selected with care and love and
even hope—and brought to this apartment and arranged

9

with taste and pride.

That was a long time ago. Now the once loved pattern of the couch upholstery has to fight to show itself from under acres of crocheted doilies and couch covers which have themselves finally come to be more important than the upholstery. And here a table or a chair has been moved to disguise the worn places in the carpet; but the carpet has fought back by showing its weariness, with depressing uniformity, elsewhere on its surface.

Weariness has, in fact, won in this room. Everything has been polished, washed, sat on, used, scrubbed too often. All pretenses but Living itself have long since vanished from the very atmosphere of this room.

Moreover, a section of this room, for it is not really a room unto itself, though the landlord's lease would make it seem so, slopes backward to provide a small kitchen area where the family prepares the meals which are eaten in the living room proper which must also serve as dining room. The single window which has been provided for these "two" rooms is located in this kitchen area. The sole natural light which the family may enjoy in the course of a day is only that which fights its way through this little window.*

At left, a door leads to a bedroom which is shared by Mama and her daughter, Beneatha. At right opposite, is a second room (which in the beginning of life for this apartment was probably a breakfast room or something) which serves as a bedroom for Brother and his wife, Ruth. This room may be lit through scrim.

Somewhere in the apartment is a photo of Big Walter, whose spirit suffuses the play.

---

*Ideally, the set should also suggest, if possible, the outer world of blighted tenements, clotheslines, fire escapes, etc.

A Raisin in the Sun

ACT ONE

Scene 1

Time: *The early 1950's.*

Place: *Chicago's Southside.*

At Rise: *It is morning dark in the living room.
TRAVIS snores, asleep on the makedown bed at C.,
WALTER in his and RUTH's bedroom at R. An alarm
clock sounds in bedroom. RUTH rises from bed, shuts
off alarm; raises the window shade, closes window;
shivers; puts on robe, slippers; grabs TRAVIS' shirt,
towel, toothbrush, glass and clock. She opens the door
to living room, crosses to sofa, shakes TRAVIS, places
his towel and shirt on back of sofa, clock and glass on
buffet U.R. She crosses to kitchen, raises the shade,
closes window, washes face. She calls to TRAVIS in a
slightly muffled voice between yawns: Ad lib.:* "Wake
up, Travis!" "Come on now, boy!" *He pulls pillow over
his head.*

*RUTH is about thirty. We can see that she was a
pretty girl, but now it is apparent that life has been little
she expected and disappointment has begun to hang in
her face. In a few years, before thirty-five even, she will
be known among her people as a "settled woman." This
does not mean she lacks spirit or strength. She is a*

11

woman in the middle, torn between the needs and dreams of others, and she subordinates herself because, caring deeply about theirs, she chooses to; but underneath is a fire that will erupt as needs be. For her this is no ordinary morning and, once or twice in the course of it, we should clearly see — as weakness engulfs her and she catches herself in the effort to hide it — that something is wrong. Yet even as she confronts the momentous decision that cannot be put off, she is driven by the necessity to get son and husband up and fed and out within half an hour; the best she can do is to steel herself, plunge ahead and get through it. She crosses to her son and sits him up, still asleep, crosses to C. door. He flops back. She gets milk and newspaper from hall, crosses back to give TRAVIS a good, final, rousing shake.

RUTH. Come on now, boy, it's seven-thirty! *(hits TRAVIS on butt, puts milk and paper on buffet)* I say hurry up, Travis! You ain't the only person in the world got to use a bathroom! *(She gets him to his feet, piles his shirt, towel, toothbrush and glass in his arms and crosses away. TRAVIS, asleep on his feet, does not move. She comes back and pushes him out the door to bathroom which is in the outside hall. RUTH picks up newspaper, notes WALTER is still asleep, crosses to the bedroom door and calls in to her husband.)* WALTER LEE— it's after seven-thirty! Lemme see you do some waking up in there now! *(She crosses to kitchen, puts water on to boil, heats coffee-pot. She waits.)* You better get up from there, man! It's after seven-thirty, I tell you. *(WALTER groans and covers his head. She sets table.)* All right, you just go ahead and lay there and next thing you know Travis be finished and Mr. Johnson'll be in there and you'll be fussing and cussing round here like a madman! And be late, too—! *(She waits.*

At the end of her patience she crosses to bedroom.)
WALTER LEE—it's time for you to GET UP!

(WALTER sits bolt upright. She pulls the door to and crosses back to kitchen. She puts mixing bowl and fork on sink edge, gets eggs from icebox. The bedroom door at R. opens and her husband stands in the doorway in his pajamas, which are rumpled and mismatched. He holds his clothes and toilet articles. He is a lean, intense young man in his middle thirties, inclined to quick movements and erratic speech habits—and always in his voice, indictment. As he enters RUTH runs her fingers through her sleep-disheveled hair in a vain effort and ties an apron around her housecoat.)

WALTER. (*enters and crosses in to* C.) Is he out yet—?

RUTH. What you mean, out? He ain't hardly got in there good yet.

WALTER. (*still more oriented to sleep than to a new day*) Well, what was you doing all that yelling for if I can't even get in there yet? (*crosses* R. *back of sofa to bedroom door* R., *stops and thinks*) Check coming today?

RUTH. (*gets eggs from the icebox and breaks them in bowl*) They *said* Saturday and this is just Friday and I hopes to God you ain't going to get up here first thing this morning and start talking to me 'bout no money—'cause I 'bout don't want to hear it.

WALTER. (*crosses in to* C.) Something the matter with you this morning?

RUTH. No—I'm just sleepy as the devil. What kind of eggs you want?

WALTER. Not scrambled. (*RUTH beats eggs. WAL-TER notes her action, then puts his clothes on* L. *end of sofa.*) Paper come? (*RUTH points impatiently to the rolled up* Tribune *on the table, and he gets it and spreads it out and vaguely reads the front page.*) [Set off another A-bomb yesterday.

RUTH. (*maximum indifference*) Did they?

WALTER. (*looking up*) What's the matter with you?

RUTH. Ain't nothing the matter with me. And don't keep asking me.

WALTER. Ain't nobody bothering you.] (*reading the news absently again*) Say Colonel McCormick is sick.

RUTH. (*puts egg bowl back in icebox; affecting tea party interest*) Is he now? Po' thing.

WALTER. (*sighing and looking at alarm clock*) Now what is that boy doing in that bathroom all this time? He is just going to have to start getting up earlier. I can't be being late to work on account of him fooling around in there. (*He rises, crosses up to door.*)

RUTH. (*pours and stirs oats in hot water*) Oh, no, he ain't going to be getting up no earlier no such thing! It ain't his fault that he can't get to bed 'cause he got a bunch of crazy good-for-nothing clowns running their mouths in what is supposed to be his bedroom after ten o'clock at night —

WALTER. (*crosses back of kitchen table, gets a cigarette from Ruth's handbag hanging on the back of the chair* L.) That's what you're mad about, ain't it? (*topping her*) The things I want to talk about with my friends just couldn't be important in your mind, could they? (*He crosses to kitchen window and looks out, smoking and enjoying his first one deeply.*)

RUTH. (*crosses to table for milk; almost matter-of-factly, a complaint too automatic to deserve emphasis*)

Why you always got to smoke before you eat in the morning?

WALTER. (*at the window*) Just look at 'em down there—running and racing to work—(*He turns and faces his wife and watches her a moment at the stove. RUTH mixes milk in the eggs. Appreciatively, with sudden softness:*) You look young this morning, Baby. *(He crosses to RUTH.)*

RUTH. (*Utter indifference*) Yeah?

WALTER. Just for a second—stirring them eggs. Just for a second it was—you looked real young again. *(He reaches for her; she stiffens, takes milk to table, pours a glass for TRAVIS. Drily:)* It's *gone* now—you look like yourself again!

RUTH. (*scrapes cereal into bowl*) Man, if you don't shut up and leave me alone.

WALTER. (*looking out to the street again*) First thing a man ought to learn in life is not to make love to no colored woman first thing in the morning. Y'all some eeeevil people at eight o'clock in the morning.

(*TRAVIS appears in the hall doorway almost fully dressed and quite wide-awake now, his towel and pajamas across his shoulders. He is a sturdy, handsome little boy of ten or eleven. He opens the door and signals for his father to make the bathroom in a hurry. WALTER starts to sit, springs up as TRAVIS enters. RUTH puts cereal bowl on the table, pours milk on the cereal.*)

TRAVIS. (*watching the bathroom*) Daddy, come on!

(*WALTER gets his bathroom utensils and flies out to the bathroom.*)

RUTH. Sit down and have your breakfast, Travis. (*She gets butter from icebox.*)

TRAVIS. (*puts slippers L. end of sofa, toothbrush, glass on table. Then he gets his chair from L. wall and places it R. of table.*) Mama, this is Friday. (*gleefully*) Check coming tomorrow, huh?

RUTH. (*puts butter on his cereal*) You get your mind off money and eat your breakfast. (*takes butter to stove, puts some in frying pan*)

TRAVIS. (*eating*) This is the morning we supposed to bring the fifty cents to school.

RUTH. Well, I ain't got no fifty cents this morning.

TRAVIS. Teacher say we have to.

RUTH. I don't care what teacher say. I ain't got it. Eat your breakfast, Travis.

TRAVIS. I *am* eating.

RUTH. Hush up now and just eat!

TRAVIS. (*He gives her an exasperated look and eats grudgingly.*) You think Grandmama would have it?

RUTH. No! And I want you to stop asking your grandmother for money, you hear me?

TRAVIS. (*outraged*) Gaaaleee! I don't ask her, she just gimme it sometimes!

RUTH. (*under breath almost*) TRAVIS WILLARD YOUNGER—I got too much on me this morning to be—

TRAVIS. Maybe Daddy—

RUTH. TRAVIS!

(*TRAVIS hushes abruptly. They are both quiet and tense for several seconds. RUTH puts the butter in the icebox.*)

TRAVIS. (*presently*) Could I maybe go carry some groceries in front of the supermarket after school, then?

RUTH. Just hush, I said. (*TRA VIS jabs his spoon into his cereal bowl viciously and rests his head in anger upon his fists.*) If you're through eating you can make up your bed.

TRAVIS. (*obeys stiffly and rises from the table, crosses the room angrily to the bed and more or less folds the bedclothes in a heap. He gets school books and cap from buffet. He crosses to C. door. Sulking and standing apart from her unnaturally:*) I'm gone.

RUTH. (*Looking up from the stove to inspect him automatically, she crosses to her handbag on chair L. of table.*) Come here. (*He crosses to her and she studies his head.*) If you don't take this comb and fix this here head you better! (*TRA VIS puts down his books with a great sigh of oppression and returns D.R. to the mirror. His mother mutters under her breath about his "slubbornness."*) 'Bout to march out of here with that head looking like chickens slept in it! I just don't know where you get your slubborn ways.

TRAVIS. (*With conspicuously brushed hair he gets his jacket angrily and crosses to C. door.*) I'm gone.

RUTH. (*pours eggs into pan, puts egg bowl in the sink*) And get your jacket, too. Looks chilly out this morning. Get your carfare and milk money—(*He finds her handbag and fishes in it. She waves one finger.*) and not one penny for no caps, you hear me?

TRAVIS. (*with sullen politeness:*) Yes'm.

(*He tosses back a coin and we hear the clink; turns in outrage to leave, crosses U.C. again to door. RUTH watches him as he approaches the door almost comically in his frustration. When she speaks to him her voice has become a very gentle tease.*

RUTH. (*at* R. *end of sink, mocking; as she thinks TRAVIS would say it*) Oh, Mama makes me so mad sometimes I don't know what to do! (*TRAVIS stands at the door and RUTH waits and continues to his back as he stands stock still in front of the door.*) I wouldn't kiss that woman good-bye this morning not for nothing in this world! (*TRAVIS finally turns around and rolls his eyes at her knowing the mood has changed and he is vindicated; he does not, however, move toward her yet.*) Not for nothing in this world! (*She finally holds out her arms, he hesitates a long moment, and we see that it is a way between them very old and practiced. TRAVIS crosses* D.C. *and allows her to embrace him warmly but keeps his face fixed with masculine rigidity. She holds him back from her presently, and looks at him and runs her fingers over the features of his face. With utter gentleness:*) Now — whose little old angry man are you?

TRAVIS. (*The masculinity and gruffness start to fade at last.*) Aw Gaalee — Mama —

RUTH. (*mimicking*) Aw — Gaaaalleeeeee, Mama! (*She pushes him with rough playfulness and finality toward the door.*) Get on out of here or you going to be late.

TRAVIS. (*Crosses to* C. *door. In the face of love, new aggressiveness:*) Mama, could I please go carry groceries?

RUTH. (*stirs eggs in pan*) Honey, it's starting to get so cold evenings.

WALTER. (*coming in from the bathroom, crosses* R. *into his bedroom with his pajamas, towel, toothbrush and glass*) What is it he wants to do?

RUTH. Go carry groceries at the supermarket.

WALTER. Well, let him go —

TRAVIS. (*quickly to the ally; crosses* R. *to bedroom door*) I *have* to — she won't gimme the fifty cents —

WALTER. (*re-enters from bedroom; to his wife only:*) Why not—?

RUTH. (*simply and with flavor*) 'Cause we don't have it.

WALTER. (*to RUTH only as he crosses to* C.) What you tell the boy things like that for? (*reaching down on the line into his pants' pocket with a rather important gesture, turns, crosses down in front of sofa*) Here, son—(*He hands the boy the coin, but his eyes are only on his wife. TRAVIS takes the money happily.*)

TRAVIS. Thanks, Daddy. (*He starts out.*)

(*RUTH watches both of them with murder in her eyes. WALTER stares back at her with defiance and suddenly reaches out for his son and into his pocket again on an afterthought.*)

WALTER. (C.L. *of sofa; without even looking at his son, still staring hard at his wife*) In fact, here's another fifty cents—Buy yourself some fruit today—or take a taxi-cab to school or something!

TRAVIS. Whoopee—

(*RUTH starts serving eggs. TRAVIS leaps up and clasps his father around the middle with his legs and they face each other in mutual appreciation; slowly WALTER peeks around the boy to catch the ultra violent rays from his wife's eyes and draws his head back as if shot.*)

WALTER. You better get down now—and get to school, man.

TRAVIS. (*at the door*) O.K. Good-bye. (*He exits.*)

WALTER. (*after him, pointing with pride; crosses* D.R. *to mirror*) That's *my* boy. (*RUTH looks at him in disgust and turns back to her work.*) You know what I was thinking 'bout in the bathroom this morning—?

RUTH. No.

WALTER. How come you always try to be so pleasant!

RUTH. What is there to be pleasant 'bout! (*She serves eggs at the table.*)

WALTER. You want to know what I was thinking 'bout in the bathroom or not!

RUTH. I know what you was thinking 'bout.

WALTER. (*ignoring her*) 'Bout what me and Willy Harris was talking about last night.

RUTH. (*pours two cups of coffee; immediately—a refrain*) Willy Harris is a good for nothing loud mouth.

WALTER. (*crosses C. to front of sofa*) Anybody who talks to me has got to be a good for nothing loud mouth, ain't he? And what you know about who's a good for nothing loud mouth? Charlie Atkins was just a "good for nothing loud mouth" too, wasn't he! When he wanted me to go in the dry-cleaning business with him. And now—he's grossing $100,000 a year. $100,000 a year! You still call *him* a loud mouth?!

RUTH. (*sits L. of table, bitterly*) Oh, Walter Lee—(*She folds her head over on her arms*).

WALTER. (*coming to her and massaging her neck sympathetically*) You tired, ain't you? Tired of everything. Me, the boy, the way we live—this beat up hole—everything. Ain't you? (*She doesn't look up, doesn't answer and resentment rises in him again.*) So tired—moaning and groaning all the time but you wouldn't do nothing to help, would you? You couldn't be on my side that long for nothing, could you?

RUTH. Walter, please leave me alone.

WALTER. A man needs for a woman to back him up—

RUTH. Walter—

WALTER. Mama would listen to you. You know she listen to you more than she do me and Bennie. She think more of you. All you have to do is just sit down with her when you drinking your coffee and talking 'bout things like you do and—(*He sits and demonstrates graphically what he thinks her methods and tone should be.*) You just sip your coffee, see, and say easy like that you been thinking 'bout that deal Walter Lee is so interested in, 'bout the store and all, and sip some more coffee, like what you saying ain't that important to you. And the next thing you know she listening good and asking you questions and when I come home—I can tell her the details. This ain't no fly-by-night proposition, Baby. I mean we figured it out, me, Willy and Bobo.

RUTH. (*with a frown*) Bobo—?

WALTER. (*sits at chair above table*) Yeah. You see, this little liquor store cost $75,000 and we figured the initial investment on the place be 'bout $30,000, see. Ten thousand each. Course, there's a couple of hundred you got to pay so's you don't spend your life waiting for them clowns to get your license approved—

RUTH. You mean graft?

WALTER. (*frowning impatiently*) Don't call it that. See there, that just goes to show you what women understand about the world. Baby, don't *nothing* happen for you in this world 'less you pay *somebody* off!

RUTH. Walter, leave me alone! (*She raises her head on the line, and stares at him vigorously—then says more quietly:*) Eat your eggs, they gonna be cold.

WALTER. (*straightening up from her and looking off*) You see that? Man says to his woman: I got me a dream. His woman say: Eat your eggs. (*sadly, but gaining in power*) Man say: I got to take hold of this here world, Baby! And a woman will say: Eat your eggs and go to work. Man say—(*passionately now*) I got to change my life, I'm choking to death, Baby! And his woman say—(*in utter anguish as he brings his fists down on his thighs*) Your eggs is getting cold!

RUTH. (*softly*) Walter, that ain't none of our money.

WALTER. (*not listening at all or even looking at her*) This morning, I was lookin' in the mirror and thinking about it—I'm thirty-five years old; I been married eleven years and I got a boy who sleeps in the living-room—and all I got to give him is nothing. Nothing but stories about how rich white people live—

RUTH. Eat your eggs, Walter.

WALTER. (*rises, slamming the table*) DAMN MY EGGS—DAMN ALL THE EGGS THAT EVER WAS!

RUTH. Then go to work.

WALTER. (*looking up at her, crosses L. to above table*) See—I'm trying to talk to you 'bout me—(*shaking his head with the repetition*) And all you can say is eat them eggs and go to work.

RUTH. (*wearily*) Honey, you never say nothing new. I listen to you every day—every night and every morning and you never say nothing new. (*shrugging*) So you would rather *be* Mr. Arnold than be his chauffeur. So—I would *rather* be living in Buckingham Palace.

WALTER. That is just what is wrong with the colored woman in this world—don't understand about building their men up and making 'em feel like they somebody. Like they can do something.

RUTH. (*drily, but to hurt*) There *are* colored men who do things.

WALTER. No thanks to the colored woman.

RUTH. (*boiling over*) Well, being a colored woman I guess I can't help myself none! (*She crosses to closet for ironing board, sets it up behind the sofa, attacks a huge pile of rough dried clothes, sprinkling them in preparation for ironing and rolling them into balls.)*

WALTER. We one group of men tied to a race of women with small minds.

(His sister BENEATHA enters on the line and WALTER regards her in dismay: in pajamas or red flannel nightgown and with her long thick hair standing up wildly or in hideous curlers, she is a "sight." BENEATHA is about twenty, as slim and intense as her brother. She is not as pretty as her sister-in-law, but her lean, almost intellectual face has a handsomeness of its own. She passes through the room without looking at either of them to the outside door and looks, a little blindly, out to the bathroom. She sees that it has been lost to the Johnsons and closes the door with a sleepy vengeance.)

BENEATHA. *(Her speech is a mixture of many things; it is different from the rest of the family's insofar as education has permeated her sense of English — and perhaps the midwest rather than the south has finally — at last — won out in her inflection; but not altogether because over all of it is a soft slurring and transformed use of vowels which is the decided influence of the Southside.)* I am going to start timing those people. *(sits in armchair)*

WALTER. You should get up earlier.

BENEATHA. *(Her face is in her hands—she is still fighting the urge to go back to bed.)* Really—would you suggest dawn? Where's the paper? *(Still preoccupied with RUTH and his failed effort to win her over, he brings it, but as she reaches for it, drops it past her hand to floor. With a look, she picks it up.)*

WALTER. (*surveying her*) You are one horrible-looking chick at this hour.

BENEATHA. (*drily*) Good morning, everybody!

WALTER. (*senselessly*) How is school coming?

BENEATHA. (*in the same spirit*) Lovely. Lovely. And you know, Biology is the greatest. Yesterday I dissected something that — (*looking up at him as the sarcasm builds to a final sharp thrust*) looked just like *you!*

WALTER. I just wondered if you've made up your mind and everything.

BENEATHA. (*gaining in sharpness and impatience prematurely*) And what did I answer yesterday morning — and the day before that — ?

RUTH. (*crossing back to ironing board R., like someone disinterested and old*) Don't be so nasty, Bennie.

BENEATHA. (*still to her brother*) And the day before that and the day before that!

WALTER. (*defensively*) I'm interested in you. Something wrong with that? Ain't many girls who decide —

WALTER and BENEATHA. (*in unison*) — "to be a doctor."

(*Silence. She withdraws into newspaper.*)

WALTER. Have we figured out yet just exactly how much medical school is going to cost?

BENEATHA. (*flings down the paper, exits to bathroom, knocks*) COME ON OUT OF THERE, PLEASE! (*reenters*)

RUTH. Walter Lee, why don't you leave that girl alone and get out of here to work?

WALTER. (*looking at his sister intently*) You know the check is coming tomorrow.

BENEATHA. (*turning on him with maddening restraint.*

She crosses D.R. *and sprawls on sofa.*) That money belongs to Mama, Walter, and it's for her to decide how to use it. I don't care if she wants to buy a house or a rocket ship or just nail it up and look at it—it's hers. Not ours—*hers.*

WALTER. (*bitterly*) Now ain't that fine! You just got your mother's interests at heart, ain't you, girl? You such a nice girl—but Mama can always take a few thousand and help you through school— can't she?

BENEATHA. I have never asked anyone around here to do anything for me.

WALTER. No! But the line between asking and just accepting when the time comes is big and wide—ain't it!

BENEATHA. (*with fury*) What do you want from me, Brother—that I quit school or just drop dead, which!

WALTER. I don't want nothing but for you to stop acting holy around here—me and Ruth done made some sacrifices for you—why can't you do something for the family?

RUTH. Walter, don't be dragging me in it.

WALTER. You are in it—Don't you get up and go work in somebody's kitchen to help put clothes on her back—?

(*BENEATHA rises, crosses, sits armchair* D.R.)

RUTH. Oh, Walter—that's not fair—

WALTER. It ain't that nobody expects you to get on your knees and say thank you, Brother! (*Waving his arms and bowing up and down*) Thank you, Ruth; thank you, Mama —and thank you, Travis, for wearing the same pair of shoes for two semesters—

BENEATHA. (*jumping up*) WELL—I DO—ALL RIGHT?- THANK EVERYBODY! (*falls on her knees*) AND FOR- GIVE ME FOR EVER WANTING TO BE ANYTHING AT ALL! (*pursuing him on her knees across the floor*)

FORGIVE ME, FORGIVE ME, FORGIVE ME! (*She rises, crosses* D.R. *to armchair.*)

RUTH. Please stop it! Your Mama'll hear you.

WALTER. (*racing after her*) Who the hell told you you had to be a doctor? If you so crazy 'bout messing round with sick people—then go be a nurse like other women—or just get married and shut up! (*At the last words, he realizes he has gone too far.*)

BENEATHA. (*quietly, hurt*) Well—you finally got it said— It took you three years but you finally got it said. Walter, give up; leave me alone—it's Mama's money.

WALTER. HE WAS MY FATHER, TOO!

BENEATHA. So what? He was mine, too—and Travis' grandfather—But the insurance money belongs to Mama. Picking on me is not going to make her give it to you to invest in any liquor stores —(*sits; under her breath*) And I for one say, God bless Mama for that! (*On BENEATHA's line RUTH crosses* U.L. *to closet.*)

WALTER. (*to RUTH*) See—did you hear?—Did you hear!

RUTH. (*crosses* D.C. *to WALTER with WALTER's jacket from the closet*) Honey, please go to work.

WALTER. (*back of sofa, crosses* U.C. *to door*) Nobody in this house is ever going to understand me.

BENEATHA. (*as he is halfway out the door, drily*) Because you're a nut.

WALTER. (*stops, turns* D.C.) Who's a nut?

BENEATHA. You—you are a nut. Thee is mad, boy.

WALTER. (*looking at his wife and sister from the door, very sadly*) The world's most backward race of people and that's a fact. (*starts out*)

BENEATHA. (*turning slowly in her chair*) And then there are all those prophets who would lead us out of the wilderness—(*Rises, crosses* U.C. *WALTER slams out of the house. She opens door and yells after him.)* Into the swamps! *(shuts it and sits)*

RUTH. Bennie, why you always gotta be pickin' on your brother? Can't you be a little sweeter sometimes?

(BENEATHA looks at her in disbelief, finds textbook and pencil and sits. Door opens. WALTER walks in.)

WALTER. *(looking from RUTH to BENEATHA to the floor)* I—uh— *(He fumbles in great embarrassment, clears throat, looks at BENEATHA who pretends not to listen, half whispers:)* I need some money—*(finally blurts)*—for carfare.

RUTH. *(looks at him, then warms, teasing, but tenderly)* Fifty cents? *(She gets her purse from handbag.)* Here. *(kisses his cheek and presses dollar into his hand)* Take a taxi!

(WALTER exits unamused. MAMA enters L. She is a woman in her early sixties, full-bodies and strong. She is one of those women of certain grace and beauty who wear it so unobtrusively that it takes a while to notice. Her dark brown face is surrounded by the total whiteness of her hair—and—being a woman who has adjusted to many things in life and overcome many more, her face is full of strength. She has, we can see, wit and faith of a kind that keep her eyes lit and full of interest and expectancy. She is, in a word, a beautiful woman. Her bearing is perhaps most like that of the Herero women—rather as if she imagines that as she walks she bears a basket or a vessel upon her head. Her speech on the other hand is as careless as her carriage is precise—she is inclined to slur everything—but the voice is perhaps not so much quiet as simply—soft.)

MAMA. Who that round here slamming doors at this hour? (*She crosses through the room, fixing a bandana on her head in honor of the forthcoming labors of the day. She goes to the window, opens it and brings in a feeble little plant growing doggedly in a small pot on the window sill. She feels the dirt.*)

RUTH. That was Walter Lee. He and Bennie was at it again.

MAMA. (*takes the plant to the sink, waters it*) My children and they tempers. Lord, if this little old plant don't get more sun than it's been getting it ain't never going to see Spring again. What's the matter with you this morning, Ruth, you looks right peaked. You aiming to iron all them things—leave some for me. Bennie honey, it's too drafty for you to be sitting round half dressed. Where's your robe?

BENEATHA. (*reading*) In the cleaners.

MAMA. Well, go get mine.

BENEATHA. I'm not cold, Mama, honest.

MAMA. I know—but you so thin—

BENEATHA. (*irritably*) Mama, I'm not cold.

MAMA. (*seeing the makedown bed as TRAVIS has sloppily left it; crosses R. to sofa*) Lord have mercy, look at that poor bed. Bless his heart—he tries, don't he?

RUTH. (*crosses L. to sink above table with piece of laundry, tries rubbing out a spot under the faucet*) No—he don't half try at all 'cause he knows you going to come along behind him and fix everything. That's just how come he don't know how to do nothing right now—you done spoiled that boy so.

MAMA. (*folds bedding*) Well—he's a little boy. Ain't supposed to know 'bout housekeeping. (*Baby talk*) My baby, that's what he is. What you fix for his breakfast?

RUTH. (*angrily*) I feed my son Lena!

MAMA. *(emphatically)* I ain't meddling. *(Pause. Underbreath)* I just noticed all last week he had cold cereal. When it starts getting this chilly a child ought to have some hot grits or something when he goes out—

RUTH. *(crosses above table to ironing board, furious)* I gave him hot oats—is that all right?

MAMA. I ain't meddling. *(Pause. Carrying bedding u.r.)* Put a lot of nice butter on it? *(RUTH shoots her an angry look and does not reply. Pause.)* He likes lots of butter. *(exits bedroom)*

RUTH. (*exasperated*) Lena—

MAMA. *(re-enters; to BENEATHA. She is inclined to wander sometimes conversationally.)* What was you and your brother fussing 'bout—? *(The bathroom door slams.)*

BENEATHA. It's not important, Mama. (*She picks up her towels and rushes out.*)

MAMA. (*u.c. back of L. end of sofa*) What was they fighting about?

RUTH. Now you know as well as I do.

MAMA. (*shaking her head*) Brother still worrying hisself sick about that money?

RUTH. You know he is.

MAMA. You had breakfast?

RUTH. Some coffee.

MAMA. (*crosses to RUTH*) Girl, you better start eating and looking after yourself better. You almost thin as Travis. (*crosses into kitchen area to the sink L. with some dishes*)

RUTH. Lena—

MAMA. Un-hunh?

RUTH. What are you going to do with it?

MAMA. Now don't you start, child. It's too early in the morning to be talking about money. Besides, it ain't

Christian.

RUTH. It's just that he got his heart set on that store —

MAMA. (*She crosses above table, sits* R. *of table with coffee cup.*) We ain't no business people, Ruth. We just plain working folks.

RUTH. (*still at ironing board behind sofa*) Ain't nobody business people till they go into business. Walter Lee says colored people ain't never going to start getting ahead till they start gambling on some different kinds of things in the world — investments and things.

MAMA. What done got into you, girl? Walter Lee done finally sold you on investing?

RUTH. No. Mama, something is happening between Walter and me. I don't know what it is — but he *needs* something — something I can't give him any more. He needs this chance, Lena.

MAMA. (*frowning deeply*) But liquor, honey —

RUTH. (*above sofa, sprinkling laundry*) Well — like Walter say — I 'spec' people going to always be drinking themselves some liquor.

MAMA. Well — whether they drinks it or not ain't none of my business. But whether I sells it to 'em is — and I don't want that (*emphatically, hand up*) on my ledger this late in life. (*stopping suddenly and studying her daughter-in-law*) Ruth Younger, what's the matter with you today? You look like you could fall over right there.

RUTH. I'm tired.

MAMA. Then you better stay home from work.

RUTH. I can't stay home. She be calling up the agency — "My girl didn't come in today — send me somebody! My girl didn't come in!" Oh, she just have a fit —

MAMA. Well, let her have it. I'll just call her up and say you get the flu —

RUTH. (*laughing*) Why the flu?

MAMA. 'Cause it sounds respectable to 'em. Something white people get, too. They know 'bout the flu. (*A beat.*) Otherwise they think you been cut up or something when you tell 'em you sick.

RUTH. I got to go in. We need the money.

MAMA. (*rises, crosses* D.L. *to sink with TRAVIS' milk glass*) Lord, have mercy! Somebody would of thought my children done all but starved to death the way they talk about money here late. Child, we got a great big old check coming tomorrow.

RUTH. (*crosses* L. *to* C. *sincerely—but also self-right-eously*) Now that's your money. It ain't got nothing to do with me. We all feel like that—Walter and Bennie and me—even Travis.

MAMA. (*gets toast from oven; thoughtfully and suddenly very far away*) Ten thousand dollars—(*She fingers her plant on* R. *edge of sink.*)

RUTH. Sure is wonderful.

MAMA. (*crosses* R. *to table and sits*) Ten thousand dollars.

RUTH. (*crosses in to MAMA to* L. *of kitchen table*) You know what you should do, Miss Lena? You should take yourself a trip somewhere. To Europe or South America or someplace—

MAMA. (*throwing up her hands at the thought*) Oh, child!

RUTH. I'm serious. Just pack up and leave! Forget about the family and have yourself a ball for once in your life—

MAMA. (*still sitting kitchen table, pungently*) You sound like I'm just about ready to die. Who'd go with me? What I look like wandering 'round Europe by myself?

RUTH. *(crossing to ironing board back of sofa)* Shoot—these here—*(striking a highfalutin pose)*—rich white women do it all the time. They don't think nothing of packing up they suitcases and piling on one of them big steamships and—swoosh!—they gone, child.

MAMA. Something always told me I wasn't no rich white woman!

RUTH. Well—what are you going to do with it, then?

MAMA. I ain't rightly decided. *(thinking, and she says this with emphasis:)* Course, some of it got to be put away for Beneatha's medical schoolin'—ain't nothing going to touch that part. Nothing. *(She waits several seconds trying to make up her mind about something and looks at RUTH a little tentatively before going on.)* Been thinking that we maybe could meet the notes on a little old two-story somewhere with a yard where Travis could play in the summertime—if we use part of the insurance for a down payment and everybody kind of pitch in. I could maybe take on a little day work again—

RUTH. *(studying her mother-in-law furtively and concentrating on her ironing, anxious to encourage without seeming to)* Well, lord knows, we've put enough rent into this here rat trap to pay for four houses by now—

MAMA. *(Still sitting R. of kitchen table. She looks up at the words "rat trap" and RUTH wishes she could take them back.)* "Rat trap"—*(MAMA looks around and leans back and sighs—in a sudden reflective mood—.)* yes, that's all it is. *(smiling)* I remember just as well the day me and Big Walter moved in here though. Hadn't been married but two weeks and wasn't planning on living here no more than a year. *(She shakes her head at the dissolved dream.)* We was going to set away, little by little, don't you know, and buy a little place out in Morgan Park. Even picked out the house. (*chuckling a little*) Looks right dumpy today. But lord, child, you should know all the dreams I had 'bout buying that house and fixing it up and making me a little garden in the back — (*She waits and stops smiling.*) And didn't none of it happen.

RUTH. (*sits in chair L. of table*) Yes, life can be a barrel of disappointments, sometimes.

MAMA. Honey, Big Walter would come in here some nights back then and slump down on that couch there and just look at the rug, and look at me and look at the rug and then back at me — And I'd know he was down then — really down. (*After a second very long and thoughtful pause; she is seeing back to times that only she can see.*) And then, lord, when I lost that baby — little Claude — I almost thought I was going to lose Big Walter, too. Oh that man grieved hisself! He was one man to love his children.

RUTH. (*rises, crosses in front of table and goes U.R. to ironing board, torn by her own thoughts*) Ain't nothin' can tear at you like losin' your baby.

MAMA. I guess that's how come that man finally worked hisself to death like he done. Like he was fighting his own war with this here world that took his baby from him.

RUTH. He sure was a fine man, Mr. Younger. (*She crosses L. side of couch with socks from basket.*)

MAMA. Crazy 'bout his children! God knows there was plenty wrong with Walter Younger—hard-headed, mean, kind of wild with the women. (*With an edge of bitterness*) *Plenty* wrong with him. (*shaking it off*) But he sure loved his children. Always wanted them to have something—be something. That's where Brother gets all these notions, I reckon. Big Walter used to say, he'd get right wet in the eyes sometimes, lean his head back with the water standing in his eyes and say—(*straightening, head thrown back, looking off in re-creation of the robust voice, the poetry and pride of the man*) "Seem like God didn't see fit to give the black man nothing but dreams—but He did give us children to make them dreams seem worthwhile." (*She smiles.*) He could talk like that, don't you know.

RUTH. (*leaves socks on L. end of sofa*) Yes, he sure could. He was a good man, Mr. Younger.

MAMA. Yes, a fine man. Just couldn't never catch up with his dreams, that's all.

BENEATHA. (*She comes in brushing her hair and looking up to the ceiling where a vacuum cleaner has started up. Crosses to D.R. mirror.*) What could be so dirty on that woman's rugs that she has to vacuum them every single day?

RUTH. I wish a certain young woman 'round here who I could name would take inspiration about certain rugs in a certain apartment I could also mention.

BENEATHA. (*shrugging*) How much cleaning can a house need, for Christ's sake?

MAMA. (*not liking the Lord's name used thus*) Bennie!

RUTH. Just listen to her—just listen!

BENEATHA. Oh God!

MAMA. If you use the Lord's name just one more time—

BENEATHA. (*a bit of a whine*) Oh, Mama—

RUTH. Fresh—just fresh as salt, this girl!

BENEATHA. (*drily*) Well—if the salt loses its savor—

MAMA. (*rises, partly clears table, crosses to sink*) Now that will do. I just ain't going to have you 'round here reciting the scriptures in vain—you hear me?

BENEATHA. How did I manage to get on everybody's wrong side by just walking into a room?

MAMA. (*crosses back to table, clearing it and crosses* D.L. *to sink again*) What time you be home from school?

BENEATHA. Kind of late. Madeline is going to start my guitar lessons today. *(crosses into* L. *bedroom for quick change)*

(*MAMA and RUTH look up with the same expression.*)

MAMA. (*gets cup and saucer from shelf*) Your what kind of lessons?

BENEATHA. *(From bedroom)* Guitar.

RUTH. Oh Father!

MAMA. How come you done taken it in your mind to learn to play the guitar?

BENEATHA. *(From bedroom)* I just want to, that's all.

MAMA. (*crosses to table, wipes it, smiling*) Lord, child, don't you know what to do with yourself? How long it going to be before you get tired of this now — (*crosses* R. *to above table*) Like you got tired of that little play-acting group you joined last year? (*looking at* RUTH) And what was it the year before that — ?

RUTH. The horse-back riding club for which she bought that fifty-five dollar riding habit that's been hanging in the closet ever since!

MAMA. (*crosses to sink; to* BENEATHA) Why you got to flit so from one thing to another, baby?

BENEATHA. *(entering, dressed and hopping to pull up kneesocks)* I just want to learn to play the guitar. Is there anything wrong with that?

MAMA. (*pours cup of coffee at stove*) Ain't nobody trying to stop you. (*BENEATHA exits* L. *again.*) I just wonders sometimes why you has to flit so from one thing to another. You ain't never done nothing with all that camera equipment you brought home—*(BENEATHA enters with guitar, books, bag, sets them down.)*

BENEATHA. I don't flit! I—I experiment with different forms of expression—

RUTH. (*Deadpan skepticism*) Like riding a horse?

BENEATHA. People have to express themselves one way or another.

MAMA. What is it you want to express?

BENEATHA. (*hesitates, nonplussed*) Me! (*MAMA and RUTH look at each other, then simultaneously burst into robust laughter.*) Don't worry—I don't expect you to understand. (*gets mug, pours coffee*)

MAMA. *(to change the subject)* Who you going out with tomorrow night?

BENEATHA. (*pours milk in coffee*) George Murchison again.

MAMA. (*pleased*) Oh—you getting a little sweet on him?

RUTH. You ask me this child ain't sweet on nobody but herself—(*underbreath*) Express herself!

(They laugh. MAMA gets sewing basket from buffet, socks from sofa, sits R. of table.)

BENEATHA. Oh—I like George all right, Mama. I mean I like him enough to go out with him and stuff but—*(Crosses above sofa to get lipstick)*

RUTH. *(for devilment)* What does *and stuff* mean?

BENEATHA. Mind your own business.

MAMA. *(chuckling)* Stop picking at her now, Ruth *(suddenly seized with suspicion: in mid-chuckle and without warning:)* WHAT *DOES* IT MEAN—? (*turns to face her daughter*)

BENEATHA. (*wearily*) Oh, I just mean I couldn't ever really be serious about George. He's—he's so shallow.

RUTH. Shallow? What do you mean he's shallow? He's RICH!

MAMA. Hush, Ruth. *(sewing socks)*

BENEATHA. *(putting on lipstick at mirror)* I know he's rich. He knows he's rich, too.

RUTH. Well—what other qualities a man got to have to satisfy you, little girl?

BENEATHA. You wouldn't even begin to understand. Anybody who married Walter could not possibly understand.

MAMA. (*outraged*) What kind of way is that to talk about your brother?

BENEATHA. Brother is a flip—let's face it.

MAMA. (*to RUTH, helplessly*) What's a flip?

RUTH. *(glad to add kindling)* She's saying he's crazy.

BENEATHA. Not crazy. Brother isn't really crazy yet. He—he's an elaborate neurotic.

MAMA. Hush your mouth!

BENEATHA. As for George. Well. *(standing, leaning over table on elbows, she tears and munches a bit of toast.)* George looks good—he's got a beautiful car and he takes me to nice places and I even like him sometimes—but if the Youngers are sitting around waiting to see if their little Bennie is going to tie up the family with the Murchisons, they are wasting their time. *(sips coffee)*

RUTH. You mean you wouldn't marry George Murchison even if he asked you some day? That pretty, rich thing? Honey, I knew you was odd—

BENEATHA. No I would not marry him if all I felt for him was what I feel now. Besides, George's family wouldn't really like it.

MAMA. Why not?

BENEATHA. Oh, Mama—The Murchisons are honest-to-God-real-*live*-rich colored people, and the only people in the world who are more snobbish than rich white people are rich colored people. I thought everybody knew that. I've met Mrs. Murchison. She's a scene!

MAMA. You must not dislike people 'cause they well off, honey.

BENEATHA. Why not? It makes just as much sense as disliking people 'cause they are poor, and lots of people do that.

RUTH. (*a wisdom-of-the-ages manner; to MAMA*) Well, she'll get over some of this—

BENEATHA. Get over it? What are you talking about, Ruth? Listen, I'm going to be a doctor. I'm not worried about who I'm going to marry yet—if I ever get married. (*rises, crosses* U.L. *and gets coat and bag from closet*)

MAMA and RUTH. IF!

MAMA. Now, Bennie—

BENEATHA. (*crosses* R. *above sofa, puts coat on sofa*) Oh, I probably will—but first I'm going to be a doctor, and George, for one, still thinks that's pretty funny. I couldn't be bothered with that. I am going to be a doctor and everybody around here better understand that!

MAMA. (*crosses* D.R. *of sofa, puts rag on sofa, picks up books from floor, puts them on coffee table, kindly*) 'Course you going to be a doctor, honey, God willing.

BENEATHA. (*drily*) God hasn't got a thing to do with it.

MAMA. Beneatha—that just wasn't necessary.

BENEATHA. (*gets her coat*) Well—neither is God. I get sick of hearing about God.

MAMA. Beneatha!

BENEATHA. I mean it! I'm just tired of hearing about God all the time. What has He got to do with anything—? Does he pay tuition?

MAMA. You 'bout to get your fresh little jaw slapped!

RUTH. That's just what she needs!

BENEATHA. Why? Why can't I say what I want to around here like everybody else?

MAMA. It don't sound nice for a young girl to say things like that — you wasn't brought up that way. Me and your father went to trouble to get you and Brother to church every Sunday.

BENEATHA. (D.R.) Mama, you don't understand. It's all a matter of ideas and God is just one idea I don't accept. It's not important. I am not going out and be immoral or commit crimes because I don't believe in God. I don't even think about it. (*Carried away by her own eloquence, she drifts* D.C., *almost forgetting where she is and to whom she is speaking, in pursuit of a larger vision.*) It's just that I get tired of *Him* getting credit for all the things the human race achieves through its own stubborn effort. There simply is no blasted God — there is only Man — (*savoring each word*) and it is *he* who makes miracles! (*starts* L.C. *for books, guitar, etc.*)

MAMA. (*Absorbs this speech, studies her daughter and rises slowly from the kitchen table, crosses* D.R.C. *to where BENEATHA is standing and slaps her powerfully across the face. After, there is only silence and the daughter drops her eyes from her mother's face and MAMA is very tall before her.*) Now — you say after me, in my mother's house there is still God. (*There is a long pause and BENEATHA stares at the floor wordlessly. MAMA repeats with precision and cool emotion:*) In my mother's house there is still God.

BENEATHA. In my mother's house there is still God.

(*A long pause, then.*)

MAMA. (*walking away from her, too disturbed for triumphant posture, crosses* U.L., *pauses, turns to her daughter*) There are some ideas we ain't going to have in this house. Not long as I am still head of this family.

BENEATHA. Yes, ma'am.

(*MAMA exits* L. *to bedroom*)

RUTH. (*almost gently, with profound understanding*) Bennie, you think you a woman — but you still a little girl. What you did was childish — so you got treated like a child.

BENEATHA. I see. I also see that everybody thinks it's all right for Mama to be a tyrant. (*picks up books and heads for door*) But all the tyranny in the world will never put a God in the heavens! (*She exits.*)

RUTH.(*A beat. goes to MAMA's door.*) She said she was sorry.

MAMA. (*coming out, crosses to* C.) They frightens me, Ruth. My children.

RUTH. (*crosses to MAMA*) You got good children, Lena. They just a little off sometimes — but they're good.

MAMA. No — there's something come down between me and them that don't let us understand each other and I don't know what it is. One done almost lost his mind thinking 'bout money all the time and the other done commence to talk about things I can't seem to understand in no form or fashion. What is it that's changing, Ruth?

RUTH. (*soothingly, older than her years*) Now — you taking it all too seriously. You just got strong-willed children and it takes a strong woman like you to keep 'em in hand.

MAMA. (*crosses* D.C. *then in front of table to sink; bringing her plant in from sill and sprinkling a little water on it*) They spirited all right, my children. Got to admit they got spirit — Bennie and Walter. Like this little old plant that ain't never had enough sunshine or nothing — and look at it. (*She has her back to RUTH, who has had to stop ironing and leans against something and puts the back of her hand to her forehead.*)

RUTH. (*crosses to R. kitchen chair; trying to keep MAMA from noticing*) You — sure — loves that little old thing, don't you —

MAMA. Well, I always wanted me a garden like folks had down home. This plant is close as I ever got to having one. (*She looks out of the window as she replaces the plant.*) Lord, ain't nothing as dreary as the view from this window on a dreary day, is there? Why ain't you singing this morning, Ruth? Sing that *No Ways Tired.* That song always lifts me up so—(*She turns at last to see that RUTH has slipped quietly to the floor, in a state of semi-consciousness. Crossing to her.*) Ruth! Ruth honey—what's the matter with you—Ruth!

CURTAIN

SCENE 2

A spirited Gospel number* on radio fills the apartment as the lights come up. It is the following morning; a Saturday morning and house-cleaning is in progress at the Youngers. Furniture has been shoved hither and yon, and MAMA at icebox is giving the kitchen

---

*Two possible selections for this moment: Mahalia Jackson's "Move On Up a Little Higher" or "I'm Gonna Live The Life I Sing About in My Dreams".

area walls a washing down. BENEATHA, in shorts
or dungarees, is D.R. *spraying insecticide into the*
cracks in the walls, with a handkerchief tied around
her face. TRAVIS, the sole idle one, is leaning on
his arms looking out of the window. He crosses R.
above table to C. *door, then crosses* D.C.

TRAVIS. Grandmama, that stuff Bennie is using smells
awful. Can I go downstairs, please?

MAMA. Did you get all them chores done already? I
ain't seen you doing much.

TRAVIS. Yes'm — finished early. Where did Mama go
this morning?

MAMA. (*looking at BEANEATHA*) She had to go on a
little errand.

(*The phone rings. BEANEATHA runs to answer it and*
reaches it before WALTER, who has entered R.)

TRAVIS. Where?

MAMA. To tend to *her* business.

BEANEATHA. Haylo (*disappointed*) Yes, he is. (*Announce-*
ment to all.) It's Willie Harris again. (*She tosses phone to*
WALTER who can barely catch it.)

WALTER. (*as privately as possible*) Hello, Willy. You get
the papers from the lawyer?—No, not yet. I told you the
mailman doesn't get here till 10:30—No, I'll come there.—
Yeah! Right away. (*He hangs up, goes for coat and hat.*)

BEANEATHA. Brother, where did Ruth go?

WALTER. (*as he exits*) How should I know!

TRAVIS. Aw come on, Grandma. Can I go outside?

MAMA. Oh, I guess so. You stay right in front of the
house, though, and keep a good lookout for the
postman.

TRAVIS. (*crosses into* R. *bedroom, for ball and stickball bat*) Yes'm. (*Returning, he is confronted with irresistible target: BENEATHA's butt in the air as spraying under sofa she backs behind it towards him. He edges closer, takes careful aim — and lets her have it.*) Leave them poor little old cockroaches alone, they ain't bothering you none.

BENEATHA. I'll cockroach you, boy. (*He runs as cackling madly she swings the spray gun at him both viciously and playfully.*)

TRAVIS. Grandma! Grandma!

MAMA. (*as they circle her*) Look out there, girl, before you be spilling that stuff on that child!

TRAVIS. (*safely behind the bastion of MAMA*) That's right — look out, now! (*He exits with a cocky jive strut.*)

BENEATHA. (*sprawls on sofa, drily*) I can't imagine that it would hurt him — it has never hurt the roaches!

MAMA. Well, little boys' hides ain't as tough as Southside roaches. You better get over there behind the bureau. I seen one marching out of there like Napoleon yesterday.

BENEATHA. (*crosses* U.R. *to bureau, following instructions and then sitting down*) There's really only one way to get rid of them, Mama —

MAMA. How?

BENEATHA. Set fire to this building! (*A beat*) Mama, where did Ruth go?

MAMA. (*looking at her with meaning*) To the doctor, I think.

BENEATHA. The doctor? — What's the matter? (*They exchange glances.*) You don't think —

MAMA. (*with her sense of drama*) Now I ain't saying what I think. But I ain't never been wrong 'bout a woman, neither.

(*The phone rings.*)

BENEATHA. (*at the phone*) Hay-lo—Oh! (*pause and shout of recognition*) Well—when did you get back!— Of course I've missed you—in my way—This morning? No—housecleaning—Mama hates it if I let people come over when the house is like this—

MAMA. (*who is listening vigorously, as is her habit; emphatically*) That's right!

BENEATHA. (*shoots her a look and moves away*) You have?—Well, that's different—what is it?—Oh, what the hell, come on over—(*quickly, before MAMA can intervene*) Right, Arrividerci. (*hangs up, jubilant.*)

MAMA. (*outraged*) Who is that you inviting over here with this house looking like this? You ain't got the pride you was born with!

BENEATHA. Asagai doesn't care how houses look, Mama—he's an intellectual. (*She crosses* D.R. *to mirror.*)

MAMA. WHO—?

BENEATHA. Asagai—Joseph Asagai. He's an African boy I met on campus—He's been studying in Canada.

MAMA. What's his name?

BENEATHA. Asagai, Joseph AH-SAH-GUY—(*hugs MAMA*) He's from Nigeria.

MAMA. Oh, that's the little country that was founded by slaves way back—

BENEATHA. No, Mama—that's Liberia. (*sets lace on buffet, replaces fruitbowl*)

MAMA. (*crosses* D.L. *at icebox*) I don't think I never met no African before.

BENEATHA. (D.R. *front of sofa*) Well, do me a favor and don't ask him a whole lot of ignorant questions like do they wear clothes—

MAMA. (*crosses to above table with sponge*) Well, now, if you think we so ignorant 'round here, maybe you shouldn't bring your friends here—

BENEATHA. It's just that all anyone seems to know about when it comes to Africa is Tarzan—

MAMA. (*wiping table, indignantly*) Why should I know anything about Africa?

BENEATHA. Why do you give money at church for the missionary work?

MAMA. Well, that's to help save people.

BENEATHA. You mean save them from *heathenism*—

MAMA. (*innocently*) Yes.

BENEATHA. I'm afraid they need more salvation from the British and the French.

(*RUTH enters forlornly and pulls off her coat. They both turn to look at her.*)

RUTH. (*false cheer*) Well, I guess from all the happy faces —everybody knows.

BENEATHA. (*crosses U.R. and above sofa*) Ruth. You pregnant!?

MAMA. (*takes RUTH's coat, hangs it up in the closet*) Lord have mercy, I sure hope it's a little old girl. Travis ought to have a sister.

(*BENEATHA and RUTH give her a hopeless look for grandmotherly enthusiasm. RUTH sits in chair R. of table, puts her handbag on the table.*)

BENEATHA. (*crosses to R. of RUTH*) How far along are you?

RUTH. Two months.

BENEATHA. Did you mean to? I mean did you plan it or was it an accident?

MAMA. What do you know about planning or not planning?

RUTH. (*wearily*) She's twenty years old, Lena.

BENEATHA. Did you plan it, Ruth?

RUTH. Mind your own business.

BENEATHA. It is my business — where is he going to sleep, on the *roof*? (*There is silence behind the remark as the three women react to the sense of it.*) Gee — I didn't mean that, Ruth, honest. Gee, I don't feel like that at all. I — I think it is wonderful.

RUTH. (*dully*) Wonderful.

BENEATHA. Yes — really.

MAMA. (*looking at RUTH, worried*) Doctor say everything going to be all right?

RUTH. (*far away*) Yes — she says everything is going to be fine —

MAMA. (*immediately suspicious*) "She"? What doctor you went to? (*BENEATHA sits on sofa. MAMA worriedly hovers over RUTH.*) Ruth honey — what's the matter with you — you sick?

(*RUTH has her fists clenched on her thighs and is fighting hard to suppress a scream that seems to be rising in her.*)

BENEATHA. (*rises*) What's the matter with her, Mama?

MAMA. (*working her fingers in RUTH's shoulders to relax her*) She be all right. Women gets right depressed sometimes when they get her way. (*speaking softly, expertly, rapidly*) Now you just relax, that's right — just lean back, don't think 'bout nothing at all — nothing at all —

RUTH. I'm all right — (*The glassy-eyed look melts and then she collapses into a fit of heavy sobbing.*)

MAMA. (*helps RUTH off* R. *above sofa; to RUTH*) Come on now, honey. You need to lie down and rest a while—then have some nice hot food.

(*They exit into bedroom, RUTH's weight on her mother-in-law as the doorbell rings.*)

BENEATHA. 'Oh, my God—that must be Asagai. (*She frantically flies to the mirror to fix herself up, sniffs under her arm, turns back for a final check, and at last opens the door to a rather dramatic-looking young man in dark suit with a large package.*)

ASAGAI. Hello, Alaiyo—

BENEATHA. Hello—(*Long pause as she stands paralyzed, all her "maturity" suddenly dissolved to jello. Finally, as he peers around her:*) Well—come in. And please excuse everything. My mother was very upset about the place looking like this.

ASAGAI. (*coming into the room,* U.C.) You look disturbed—Is something wrong?

BENEATHA. (*She puts things away.*) Yes—we've all got acute ghetto-itus. (*She smiles and comes toward him.*) So—. sit down. No! Wait! (*whips spraygun off sofa out of sight and restores stacked sofa cushions from floor. As he reaches to place package on coffee table, she pulls table out from under into place. He smiles, deposits package. They regard each other and finally sit, she perched on sofa arm* R, *he sofa* L., *legs crossed. Long beat.*) So, how was Canada?

ASAGAI. (*a sophisticate*) Canadian.

BENEATHA. Asagai, I'm very glad you are back.

ASAGAI. Are you really?

BENEATHA. Yes—very.

ASAGAI. Why?—you were quite glad when I went away. What happened?

BENEATHA. You went away.

ASAGAI. Ahhhhhhhh.

BENEATHA. Before—you wanted to be so serious before there was time.

ASAGAI. How much time must there be before one knows what one feels?

BENEATHA. (*stalling this particular conversation; her hands pressed together deliberately childish*) What did you bring me—?

ASAGAI. (*indicating the package*) Open it and see.

BENEATHA. (*rises from sofa, gets package, crouches on floor by coffee table, and eagerly opens the package; drawing out the colorful robes of a Nigerian woman*) Oh, Asagai! You got them for me! How beautiful! (*holding up records*) And the records, too! (*She runs to mirror and holds the material up in front of herself.*)

ASAGAI. (*coming to her*) Wait! I shall have to teach you how to drape it properly. (*He gestures for her to raise her arms. She does. He drapes it about her low across her bosom and around behind her and in front again. She pulls it up demurely as he tucks in the end and stands back to look at her. She preens and struts grandly as she thinks a Nigerian woman might.*) Ah—Oh-pay-gay-day! Oh-bah-mu-shay! (*"Opegede! Ogbamushe!"*) You wear it well—very well—mutilated hair and all.

BENEATHA. (*turning suddenly*) My hair—what's wrong with my hair?

ASAGAI. Were you born with it like that?

BENEATHA. (*reaching up to touch it*) No—of course not. (*She looks back to the mirror, disturbed.*)

ASAGAI. (*smiling*) How then?

BENEATHA. (*embarrassed and a little demure to*

discuss the Great Hair Question) You know perfectly well how—as—as nap—crinkly as yours—that's how.

ASAGAI. And it is ugly to you that way?

BENEATHA. (*quickly*) Oh, no—not *ugly*—(*More slowly, apologetically*) But it's so hard to manage when it's, well—*raw*.

ASAGAI. And so to accommodate that—you mutilate it every week?

BENEATHA. It's not mutilation!

ASAGAI. (*laughing aloud at her seriousness*) Oh—please! I am only teasing you because you are so very serious about these things. (*He stands back from her and folds his arms across his chest as he watches her pulling her hair and frowning in the mirror.*) Do you remember the first time we met at school—? (*He laughs. Takes stage slightly* R.C) You came up to me and you said, and I thought you were the most serious little thing I had ever seen—You said, (*He imitates her.*) "Mr. Asagai—I want very much to talk with you. About Africa. You see, Mr. Asagai, I am looking for my *identity!*" (*He folds over and roars with laughter.*)

BENEATHA. (*turning to him, not laughing*) Yes—(*Her face is quizzical, profoundly disturbed.*)

ASAGAI. (*Still teasing, he crosses* R. *to her and, reaching out, takes her face in his hands and turns her profile to him.*) Well—it is true that this is not so much a profile of a Hollywood queen as perhaps a Queen of the Nile—(*A mock dismissal of the importance of the question. He crosses* L. *to* C.) But what does it matter? Assimilationism is so popular in your country.

BENEATHA. (*wheeling, passionately, sharply*) I am not an assimilationist!

ASAGAI. (*The protest hangs in the room for a moment and ASAGAI studies her, his laughter fading*) Such a

serious one. (*There is a pause between them, then:*) So—
you like the robes? You must take excellent care of
them—they are from my sister's personal wardrobe.

BENEATHA. (*with incredulity*) You—you sent all the
way home—for me?

ASAGAI. (*with charm*) For you—I would do much
more. Well, that is what I came for. I must go. (*He
crosses to* C. *door.*)

BENEATHA. (*crosses* U.R. *and above sofa to* C.) Will
you call me Monday?

ASAGAI. Yes—We have a great deal to talk about, you
and I. I mean about identity and time and all that.

BENEATHA. Time?

ASAGAI. Yes—about how much time one needs to
know what one feels.

BENEATHA. (*crosses* D.L. *of sofa to front of sofa*) You
see! You never understood that there is more than one
kind of feeling which can exist between a man and a
woman—or at least—there should be.

ASAGAI. (*shaking his head negatively but gently,
crosses* D.C. *to meet her in front of the sofa*)
No—between a man and a woman there need be only
one kind of feeling. I have that for you—Now even—
right this moment—

BENEATHA. I know—and by itself—it won't do. I can
find that anywhere.

ASAGAI. For a woman it should be enough.

BENEATHA. I know—because that's what it says in all
the novels that men write. But it isn't. Go ahead and
laugh—but I'm not interested in being someone's little
episode in America or—(*with feminine vengeance*)—
one of them! (*She removes the robe and folds it.
ASAGAI has burst into laughter again.*) That's funny as
hell, huh!

ASAGAI. It's just that every American girl I have known has said that to me. White — black — in this you are all the same. And the same speech, too!

BENEATHA. (*angrily*) Yuk, yuk, yuk! (*places folded robe in box*)

ASAGAI. It's how you can be sure that the world's most liberated women are you not liberated at all. You all *talk* about it too much!

(*They are wrapt in each other's eyes as MAMA enters and is immediately all social charm because of the presence of a guest.*)

BENEATHA. (*crosses U.R. and escorts MAMA down to ASAGAI*) Oh — Mama — this is Mr. Asagai.

MAMA. How do you do?

ASAGAI. (*total politeness to an elder*) How do you do, Mrs. Younger? Please forgive me for coming at such an outrageous hour on a Saturday.

MAMA. (*Crosses D.R. and then L. to middle front of sofa. BENEATHA follows her and stands to MAMA's R. ASAGAI is on MAMA's L.*) Well, you are quite welcome. I just hope you understand that our house — (*looking daggers at BENEATHA*) — don't *always* look like this. (*a beat; chatterish*) You must come again. I would love to hear all about—(*pause, not sure of name*)— your country. I think it's so sad the way our American Negroes don't know nothing about Africa 'cept Tarzan and all that. And all that money they pour into these churches when they ought to be helping you people over there drive out them French and Englishmen done taken away your land. (*flashes a slightly superior look at her daughter upon completion of the recitation*)

ASAGAI. (*taken aback by this sudden and acutely unrelated expression of sympathy*) Yes — yes —

MAMA. How many miles is it from here to where you come from?

ASAGAI. Many thousands.

MAMA. (*looking at him as she would WALTER*) I bet you don't half look after yourself, being away from your mama so far. I 'spec' you better come 'round here from time to time and get yourself some home-cooked meals —

ASAGAI. (*moved*) Thank you. Thank you very much.

(*They are all quiet, then:*)

ASAGAI. (*crosses* U.C.) Well — I must go. I will call you Monday, Alaiyo.

(*BENEATHA follows ASAGAI.*)

MAMA. What's that he call you?

ASAGAI. Oh — "Alaiyo" — I hope you don't mind. It is what you call a "nickname," I think. It is a Yoruba word. I am a Yoruba. (*He crosses* D.C. *between MAMA and BENEATHA.*)

MAMA. (*looking at BENEATHA*) I—I thought you said he was from—(*She struggles, at a loss for the name.*)

(*BENEATHA crosses* D.L.)

ASAGAI. (*understanding*) Nigeria is my country. Yoruba is my tribal origin —

BENEATHA. (*crossing more* D.L.) You didn't tell us what Alaiyo means — for all I know, you might be calling me *Little Idiot* or something —

ASAGAI. Well—let me see—I do not know just how to explain it. The sense of a thing can be so different when it changes languages . . .

BENEATHA. You're evading.

ASAGAI. No—really it is difficult—(*thinking*) It means—it means One for Whom Bread—Food—Is Not Enough. (*He looks at her.*) Is that all right?

BENEATHA. (*understanding, softly*) Thank you.

MAMA. (*looking from one to the other and not understanding any of it*) Well—that's nice—You must come see us again—Mr.—(*hesitates, stuck*)

ASAGAI. AH-SA-GAI—

MAMA. (*pause; still can't say it*) Yes—Do come again.

ASAGAI. Good-bye. (*He exits.*)

MAMA. (*crosses to sink for glass of water as BENEATHA whirls with joy*) Lord, that's a pretty thing just went out of here! Yes, I guess I see why we done commence to get so interested in Africa 'round here. Missionaries my Aunt Jenny! (*She crosses to RUTH's bedroom with glass and exits.*)

BENEATHA. Oh, Mama—! (*She sits on sofa, rises, picks up the Nigerian robe and holds it up to her in front of the mirror again. At first she sets the head-dress on haphazardly and then notices her hair again and clutches at it and then replaces the head-dress and struts D.S., arms upraised, elbows and wrists bent outwards, and head bobbing forward like figure on an Egyptian vase.*)

TRAVIS. (*He enters and stands regarding her mystified. Then—*) What's the matter, girl, you cracking up? (*giggles and mimics her strut.*)

(*She pulls the head-dress off and regards herself in the mirror and clutches at her hair again and squinches her eyes as if trying to imagine something. Then, suddenly, she gets her box and hurriedly prepares for going out.*)

MAMA. (*enters*) [She's resting now. Travis, baby, run next door and ask Miss Johnson to please let me have a little kitchen cleanser. This here can is empty as Jacob's kettle.

TRAVIS. I just came in.

MAMA. Do as you told. (*He exits.*] *She looks at her daughter and crosses* L. *above sofa and table to sink.*) Where you going?

BENEATHA. (*halting at the door*) To become a queen of the Nile! (*She exits in a breathless blaze of glory as RUTH appears in the bedroom doorway.*)

RUTH. Where did Bennie go?

MAMA. (*drumming her fingers*) Far as I could make out — to Egypt. Who told you to get up?

RUTH. Ain't nothing wrong with me to be lying in no bed for.

MAMA. What time is it getting to?

RUTH. Ten-twenty. And the mailman going to ring that bell this morning just like he done every morning for the last umpteen years. [(*TRAVIS comes in with jar with tiny bit of cleanser at bottom.*)

TRAVIS. She say to tell you that she don't have much.

MAMA. (*angrily*) Lord, some people I could name sure is tight-fisted! (*directing her grandson*) Mark two cans of cleanser down on the list there. If she that hard up for kitchen cleanser, I sure don't want to forget to get her none!

RUTH. Lena — maybe the woman is just short on cleanser —

MAMA. (*not listening*) — Much baking powder as she done borrowed from me all these years, she could of done gone into the baking business!] (*The bell sounds suddenly and sharply, and all three people are stunned serious and silent in mid-speech. In spite of all other conversations and distractions of the morning, this is what they have been waiting for—even TRAVIS, who looks helplessly from his mother to grandmother. RUTH is the first to come to life again. To TRAVIS:*) GET DOWN THEM STEPS, BOY!

(*She crosses* U.R. *and above sofa. TRAVIS snaps to life and flies out to get the mail.*)

MAMA. (*crosses front of table in kitchen to* C.) You mean it done really come?

RUTH. (*excited*) Oh, Miss Lena!

MAMA. (*collecting herself*) Well—I don't know what we all so excited about 'round here for. We known it was coming for months. (*sits* R. *of table*)

RUTH. That's a whole lot different from having it come and being able to hold it in your hands—a piece of paper worth ten thousand dollars—(*TRAVIS bursts back into the room, he holds the envelope high above his head like a little dancer. His face is radiant and he is breathless. The other mail is tossed carelessly on the kitchen table and he pirouettes with the envelope and deposits it with sudden slow ceremony in his grandmother's lap. She accepts it—and then—merely holds it and looks at it. RUTH crosses to behind kitchen table,* L. *of MAMA.*) Come on! Open it—Lord have mercy, I wish Walter Lee was here!

TRAVIS. (*at MAMA's* R.) Open it, Grandmama!

MAMA. (*staring at it*) Now you all be quiet. It's just a check.

RUTH. Open it—

MAMA. (*still staring at it*) Now, don't act silly—We ain't never been no people to act silly 'bout no money—

RUTH. (*swiftly*) We ain't never had none before—OPEN IT!

MAMA. (*She finally makes a good strong tear and*

pulls out the thin blue slice of paper and inspects it closely. The boy and his mother study it raptly over her shoulders.) TRAVIS! (*She is counting off with doubt.*) Is them the right amount of zeros?

TRAVIS. (*He counts them off to himself.*) Yes'm — ten thousand dollars. Gaa-lee, Grandmama, you rich.

MAMA. (*She holds out the check from her, still looking at it. Slowly her face sobers into a mask of unhappiness.*) Ten thousand dollars. (*She hands it to RUTH.*) Put it away somewhere, Ruth. (*She does not look at RUTH and her eyes seem to be seeing somewhere very far off. She rises and crosses* D.L. *to sink.*) Ten thousand dollars they give you. Ten thousand dollars.

TRAVIS. (*to his mother, sincerely*) What's the matter with grandmama — don't she want to be rich?

RUTH. (*distractedly*) You go on out and play now, baby. (*TRAVIS exits* C. *MAMA has gone back to wiping plates, humming to herself. With kind exasperation:*) You've gone and got yourself upset. (*She crosses* D.L. *above table to MAMA at sink.*)

MAMA. (*not looking at her*) I 'spec' if it wasn't for you all — I would just put that money away or give it to the church or something.

RUTH. Now what kind of talk is that? Mr. Younger would just be plain mad if he could hear you talking foolish like that.

MAMA. (*stopping and staring off*) Yes — he sure would. (*sighing*) We got enough to do with that money all right. (*She halts then and turns and looks at her daughter-in-law hard; RUTH avoids her eyes and crosses far* R. *MAMA wipes her hands with finality and starts to speak firmly to RUTH.*) Where did you go today, girl?

RUTH. To the doctor.

MAMA. (*impatiently*) Now, Ruth — you know better

than that. Old Doctor Jones is strange enough in his way but there ain't nothing 'bout him make somebody slip and call him *she* like you done this morning. (*crosses R. to RUTH*)

RUTH. Well, that's what happened—my tongue slipped.

MAMA. You went to see that woman, didn't you?

RUTH. (*defensively, giving herself away*) What woman you talking about?

MAMA. (*angrily*) That woman who—

WALTER. (*He enters in great excitement.*) Mailman come! (*to RUTH as he crosses D.C. to her at R. front of sofa*) Did it come? (*RUTH unfolds the check and lays it quietly before him; watching him intently with thoughts of her own. MAMA crosses L. to sink. WALTER sits down and grasps the check close and counts off the zeros. He turns suddenly, frantically to his mother and draws some papers out of his breast pocket.*) Mama—look, old Willy Harris put everything on paper—(*He crosses to kitchen table and lays out the legal papers.*)

MAMA. Son—I think you ought to talk to your wife—I'll go on out and leave you alone—(*Crosses up to L. bedroom door.*)

WALTER. (*brings her the legal papers above table*) I can talk to her later. Mama, look—Please!

MAMA. Son—

WALTER. WILL SOMEBODY PLEASE LISTEN TO ME TODAY!

MAMA. (*quietly*) I don't 'low no yellin' in this house, Walter Lee, and you know it—(*WALTER stares at them in frustration and starts to speak several times.*) And there ain't going to be no investing in no liquor stores.

WALTER. But, Mama, you ain't even looked at it.

MAMA. I don't aim to have to speak on that again.

(*Long pause.*)

WALTER. You ain't looked at it and you don't aim to have to speak on that again? You ain't even looked at it and *you* decided — (*crumpling his papers*) Well, *you* tell that to my boy tonight when you put him to sleep on the living-room couch! (*He picks up his coat from the sofa, crosses* U.C. *and starts out.*)

RUTH. Where are you going?

WALTER. Out!

RUTH. Where?

WALTER. Just out of this house somewhere —

RUTH. (*rises, crosses* U.C.) I'll come, too.

WALTER. I don't want you to come!

RUTH. (*crosses* U.L. *to closet for her coat*) I got something to talk to you about, Walter.

WALTER. That's too bad. (*He crosses to* C. *door.*)

MAMA. (*quietly still*) Walter Lee — (*She waits and he finally turns and looks at her.*) Sit down!

WALTER. (*slams door shut.*) I'm a grown man, Mama.

MAMA. Ain't nobody said you wasn't grown. But you still in my house and my presence. And as long as you are—you'll talk to your wife civil. (*With peremptory command*) Now sit down.

RUTH. (*hurls coat at WALTER, crossing above sofa to bedroom, suddenly*) Oh, let him go on out and drink himself to death! He makes me sick to my stomach!

WALTER. (*crosses* R. *after her, violently*) And you turn mine too, Baby—! (*He hurls the coat back at her as RUTH goes into bedroom and slams the door behind her. To MAMA:*) That was my biggest mistake—!

MAMA. (*crosses to front of sofa; still quietly*) Walter, what is the matter with you?

WALTER. (*crosses* D.R. *of sofa*) Matter with me? Ain't nothing the matter with ME!

MAMA. Yes, there is. Something eating you up like a crazy man. (*WALTER sits*) Something more than me not giving you this money. The past few years I been watching it happen to you. You get all nervous acting and kind of wild in the eyes—(*WALTER jumps up impatiently at her words, crosses* U.R. and back of sofa.) I said sit there now, I'm talking to you!

WALTER. (*circles* D.C. *around front of sofa, front of coffee table, front of armchair, sits* D.R.) Mama—I don't need no nagging at me today.

MAMA. Seem like you getting to a place where you always tied up in some kind of knot about something. But if anybody ask you 'bout it you just yell at 'em and bust out the house and go out and drink somewheres. Walter Lee, people can't live with that. Ruth's a good, patient girl in her way — but you getting to be too much. Boy, don't make the mistake of driving that girl away from you.

WALTER. Why — what she ever do for me?

MAMA. She loves you.

WALTER. (*a beat. It's useless: women will never understand a man. With deliberate restraint he rises.*) Mama— I'm going out. I want to be by myself for a while. (*heads for door*)

MAMA. I'm sorry 'bout your liquor store, son. It just wasn't the thing for us to do. That's what I want to tell you about—(*sits in armchair*)

WALTER. I got to go out, Mama—(*He reaches for the door.*)

MAMA. It's dangerous, son.

WALTER. What's dangerous?

MAMA. When a man goes outside his home to look for peace.

WALTER. (*beseechingly; crosses* D.C.) Then why can't there never be no peace in this house, then?

MAMA. You done found it in some other house?

WALTER. (*crosses* L., *slams coat down on chair* L. *of kitchen table*) No—there ain't no woman! Why do women always think there's a woman somewhere when a man gets restless? (*He picks up check from table.*) Do you know what this money means to me? Do you know what this money can do for us? Mama—Mama—I want so many things—

MAMA. Yes, son—

WALTER. I want so many things that they are driving me kind of crazy. Mama—look at me.

MAMA. I'm looking at you. You are a good-looking boy. You got a job, a nice wife, a fine boy and—

WALTER. A job. (*looks at her*) Mama, a job? I open and close car doors all day long. I drive a man around in *his* limousine and say, "Yes, sir," "No, sir," "Very good, sir," "Shall I take the drive, sir?" Mama, that ain't no kind of job—that ain't nothin' at all. (*very quietly*) Mama, I don't know if I can make you understand. (*crosses* D.R.C. *to MAMA in armchair.*)

MAMA. Understand what, baby?

WALTER. (*quietly*) Sometimes it's like I can see the

future stretched out in front of me—just plain as day. The future, Mama. Hanging over there at the edge of my days. Just waiting for me—a big, looming blank space—full of *nothing*. Just waiting for *me*. But it don't have to be. (*WALTER kneels beside her,* U.S.L. *of armchair.*) Mama—sometimes when I'm downtown driving that man around and I pass them cool, quiet-looking restaurants where them white boys are sitting back and talking 'bout things—Sitting there turning deals worth millions of dollars—sometimes I see guys don't look much older than me—

MAMA. Son—how come you talk so much 'bout money?

WALTER. (*with immense passion*) Because it is life, Mama!

MAMA. (*quietly*) Oh—(*very quietly*) So now money is life. Once upon a time freedom used to be life—now it's money.

WALTER. No—it was always money, Mama. We just didn't know about it.

MAMA. No—something has changed. (*touching his face. Not in reproof, but a genuine effort at understanding*) You something new, boy. In my time we was worried about not being lynched and getting to the North if we could and how to stay alive and still have a pinch of dignity too. Now here come you and Beneatha—talking about things we ain't never even thought about hardly, me and your daddy. You ain't satisfied or proud of nothing we done. I mean that you had a home; that we kept you out of trouble till you was grown; that you don't have to ride to work on the back of nobody's street car—You my children—but how different we done become.

WALTER. (*looks at her hopelessly, pats her hand sadly,*

giving up. He rises and starts out.) You don't understand, Mama, you just don't understand.

MAMA. Son—do you know your wife is expecting another baby? (*Pause. WALTER crosses* D.L. *above table, circles in front of table, sinking down into chair* R. *of kitchen table.*) That's what she wanted to talk to you about. This isn't for me to be telling—but you ought to know. (*She waits.*) I think Ruth is thinking 'bout getting rid of that child.

WALTER. (*slowly understanding*) No—no—Ruth wouldn't do that.

MAMA. (*crossing* L. *to sink*) When the world gets ugly enough—a woman will do anything for her family. The part that's *already living.*

WALTER. You don't know Ruth, Mama, if you think she would do that.

RUTH. (*She opens the* R. *bedroom door and stands there a little limp.*) Yes, I would, too, Walter. (*Beaten, she enters, crosses to* R. *end of sofa.*) I gave her a five-dollar down-payment.

(*There is total silence as the man stares at his wife and the mother stares at her son.*)

MAMA. (*presently; crosses above table to WALTER's* L.) Well—(*She waits.* *) Well—son, I'm waiting to hear you say something—(*The silence shouts.* *) I'm waiting to hear how you be your father's son. Be the man he was—(*Pause. She waits, he wrestles with himself but can say nothing.* *) Your wife say she going to destroy your child. And I'm waiting to hear you talk like him and say we a people who give children life, not who destroys them—I'm waiting to see you stand up and look like your daddy and say we done give up one baby to poverty and that we ain't going to give up nary another one—I'm waiting.

(*WALTER faces RUTH but can say nothing. A beat.*)

M AMA. If you a son of mine, tell her! (*WALTER turns, looks at her and starts to exit*) You—you are a disgrace to your father's memory. (*WALTER exits.*) Somebody get me my hat! (*She exits* L. *bedroom.*)

CURTAIN

---

*The breaks in this speech as MAMA waits for WALTER to speak are crucial. It must not be a continuous tirade which, in effect, drives him to defiance by denying him the chance to speak for himself. MAMA gives him the space. It is the situation itself, not she, that stills his tongue.)

ACT TWO

Scene 1

TIME: *Later—same day.*

AT RISE: *RUTH is ironing again. She has the radio going: a good loud blues or perhaps Dinah Washington's "This Bitter Earth." Presently the bedroom door opposite opens, and her mouth falls and she puts down the iron in fascination.*

RUTH. Wh. · have we got on tonight!

BENEATHA. (*Emerging, grandly, from the door L. so that we can see her thoroughly robed in the costume which Asagai brought. She parades for RUTH by crossing C., then D.C., then R., in front of sofa.*) You are looking at what a well-dressed Nigerian woman wears— (*With her hair completely hidden by the head-dress, she crosses L. to C.*) Isn't it beautiful? (*She promenades R. in front of the sofa to the radio and turns it off with an arrogant flourish.*) Enough of this assimilationist junk! (*RUTH follows her with her eyes as she goes to the phonograph and puts on a record* and turns and waits ceremoniously for the music to come up; then, with a leap and a shout.*) OCOMOGOSIAY!

(*RUTH jumps. The music comes up, a lovely Nigerian melody. BENEATHA listens, enraptured, her eyes far away—"back to the past." She begins to move,*

---

*The record is the Columbia album "Drums of Passion" by Olatunji. The album cut is "Adunde." CAUTIONARY NOTE Permission to produce this play does not include permission to use this music.

vaguely, genuinely and—as it gets good to her—with rapt seriousness and exaggerated strength. RUTH is dumbfounded. The effect, not the intent, is comic.)

RUTH. What kind of dance is that?

BENEATHA. A folk dance.

RUTH. (*"Pearl Bailey," deadpan skepticism*) What kind of folks do that, honey?

BENEATHA. It's from Nigeria. It's a dance of welcome.

RUTH. Who you welcoming?

BENEATHA. (*Going into a sensual shimmy as she moves D.C.*) The men back to the village.

RUTH. Where they been?

BENEATHA. (*stops suddenly*) How should I know— out hunting or something. (*then, swept up into the dance again*) Anyway, they are coming back now—

(*WALTER enters.*)

RUTH. Well, that's good.

BENEATHA. (*with the record*)
          Alundi, alundi·
          Alundi, alunya
          Jop pu a jeepua
          Ang gu sooooooooooo

          Ai yai yae—
          Ayehayae—alundi

(*WALTER has obviously been drinking. He leans against the door heavily and watches his sister. First with distaste, then picking up her movements in place, until at last—his eyes looking off "back to the past"—he lifts both his fists to the roof and shouts:*)

WALTER. YEAH—AND ETHIOPIA STRETCH FORTH HER ARMS AGAIN!

RUTH. (*drily, looking at him*) Yes—and Africa sure is claiming her own tonight. (*She starts ironing again, giving them both up.*)

WALTER. (*all in a drunken, dramatic shout*) Shut up! —I'm digging them drums—them drums move me! (*He makes his weaving way to his wife's face and leans in close to her*) In my heart of hearts—(*He thumps his chest.*) I am much warrior!

RUTH. (*without even looking up*) In your heart of hearts you are much drunkard.

WALTER. (*Starting to wander the room, shouting*) Me and Jomo—(*intently, in his sister's face who has stopped dancing to watch him in this unknown mood*) That's my man, Kenyatta. (*Thumping his chest*) FLAMING SPEAR! HOT DAMN! (*He is suddenly in possession of an imaginary spear spearing enemies all over the room as BENEATHA joins in the quest and the two play comically off each other.*) OCOMOGOSIAY!

BENEATHA. OCOMOGOSIAY, FLAMING SPEAR!

WALTER. THE LION IS WAKING—OWIMOWEH! (*He leaps over the coffee table, flings his "spear" at RUTH, who ducks, and possessed by a vision dramatically mounts the table and raises his arms commandingly.*)

BENEATHA. OWIMOWEH!

WALTER. (*On the table, very far gone, his eyes pure glass sheets, his posture that of Belafonte singing "Matilda" mixed with Paul Robeson at mighty pitch. He sees what we cannot, that he is a leader of his people, a great chief, a descendant of Chaka, and that the hour to march has come. Raising his arms for silence.*) LISTEN, MY BLACK BROTHERS—

BENEATHA. (*dancing closer, worshipfully*) We hear you!

WALTER. Do you hear the waters rushing against the shores of our coastlands—?

BENEATHA. OCOMOGOSIAY!

WALTER. Do you her the screeching of the cocks in yonder hills beyond where the chiefs meet in council for the coming of the mighty war—?

BENEATHA. OCOMOGOSIAY!

(*And now the lighting shifts subtly to suggest the world of WALTER's imagination and the mood shifts from pure comedy to something larger. It is the inner WALTER speaking: the South Side chauffeur has assumed an unexpected majesty. Not shouting, but savoring the images.*)

WALTER. Do you hear the beating of the wings of the birds flying low over the mountains and the low places of our land—?

BENEATHA. OCOMOGOSIAY!

WALTER. Do you hear the singing of the women, singing the war songs of our fathers to the babies in the great houses—Singing the sweet war songs—OH, DO YOU HEAR, MY *BLACK* BROTHERS! (*The doorbell rings.*)

(*RUTH shuts off the phonograph, flicks on the entry light —the lighting returns to normal—and opens door to admit GEORGE MURCHISON.*)

BENEATHA. (*completely gone*) We hear you, Flaming Spear—

WALTER. Telling us to prepare for the GREATNESS OF THE TIME!! (*to GEORGE, extending his hand for the fraternal clasp*) BLACK BROTHER—!

GEORGE. (*cooly*) Black Brother, *hell!*

RUTH. (*having had enough and embarrassed for the family,*) Beneatha, you got company— what's the matter with you? Walter Lee Younger, get down off that table and stop acting like a fool—(*WALTER manages to descend with dignity and advances hand extended, but at the last moment grabs his mouth and makes a quick exit to bathroom.*) He's had a little to drink—I don't know what her excuse is.

GEORGE. (*to BENEATHA*) Look, honey, we're going *to* the theatre—we're not going to be *in* it—so go change, huh? (*Looks at watch.*)

(*BENEATHA looks at him and slowly, ceremoniously— with pride and a quite genuine expectation of being complimented—lifts her hands and pulls off the head- dress. Her hair is close-cropped and unstraightened.* * *GEORGE freezes mid-sentence and RUTH's eyes all but fall out of her head.*)

GEORGE. What in the name of—

RUTH. (*touching BENEATHA's hair*) Girl—you done lost your natural mind!? Look at your head!

GEORGE. What have you done to your head—I mean your hair!

BENEATHA. Nothing—except cut it off.

RUTH. Now that's the truth—it's what *ain't* been done

---

*Depending on the actress's own hairstyle, BENEATHA will require a processed straightened-hair wig in Act One and/or an Afro wig in Two and Three (close-cropped or fuller as suits her features—but, above all, attractive *and natural,* not highly styled or geri-curled). The difference between the two hairdos must be immediately apparent— and for the scene to work, RUTH's contrasting traditional hairdo will also have to be unmistakably processed.

to it! You expect this boy to go out with you with your head all nappy like that?

BENEATHA. (*looking at GEORGE*) That's up to George. If he's ashamed of his heritage—

GEORGE. Oh, don't be so proud of yourself, Bennie—just 'cause you look eccentric.

BENEATHA. How can something that's natural be eccentric?

GEORGE. That's what being eccentric means—being natural. Get dressed.

BENEATHA. I don't like that, George.

RUTH. (*crosses into c. between GEORGE and BENEATHA*) Why must you and your brother make an argument out of everything people say?

BENEATHA. Because I hate assimilationist Negroes!

RUTH. Will somebody please tell me what assimila-whoever means!

GEORGE. (D.R. *front of sofa*) Oh, it's just a college girl's way of calling people Uncle Toms—but that isn't what it means at all.

RUTH. Well, what does it mean?

BENEATHA. (*cutting GEORGE off and staring at him as she replies to RUTH, crossing R. into c.*) It means someone who is willing to give up—his own culture—and submerge himself completely in the dominant and—in this case—*oppressive* culture!

GEORGE. Oh dear, dear, dear! Here we go! A lecture on the African past! On our Great West African Heritage! In one second we will hear all about the great Ashanti empires; the great Songhay civilizations and the great sculpture of Benin—and then some poetry in the Bantu—(*beats drums*) and the whole monologue will end with the word *heritage!* Let's face it, baby, your heritage is nothing but a bunch of raggedyassed spirituals and—(*pungently*) some grass huts!

BENEATHA. GRASS HUTS! (*RUTH manhandles BE-NEATHA* U.L. *to* L. *bedroom.*) See there—you are standing there in your splendid ignorance talking about people who were the first to smelt iron on the face of the earth! (*RUTH is pushing her into the door like a noisy jack-in-the-box.*) The Ashanti were performing surgical operations when the English—(*RUTH pulls the door to with BENEATHA on the other side and smiles graciously to GEORGE. BENEATHA re-enters, then exits again.*) were still tatooing themselves with blue dragons!

RUTH. Have a seat, George. (*Puts ironing board behind icebox. GEORGE sits on sofa—on a broken spring. He shifts uncomfortably, at last sits back and straightens pants crease.*) Warm, ain't it? I mean for September. (*Sits, folds hands primly on lap, determined to demonstrate the civilization of the family; pause*) Just like they always say about Chicago weather. If it's too hot or cold—just wait a minute and it'll change. (*Smiles happily at this cliche of cliches.*) Everybody says it's got to do with them bombs and things they keep setting off. (*pause*) Would you like a nice cold beer? (*crosses to icebox.*)

GEORGE. No, thank you. I don't care for beer. (*He looks at his watch.*) I hope she hurries up. (*rises.*)

RUTH. What time is the show?

GEORGE. (*turns back to RUTH* D.R., *sits on sofa again*) It's an eight-thirty curtain. That's just Chicago, though. In New York standard curtain time is eight-forty. (*He is rather proud of this knowledge.*)

(*WALTER starts from bathroom.*)

RUTH. (*properly appreciating it*) You get to New York a lot?

GEORGE. (*offhand*) Few times a year.

RUTH. Oh — that's nice. I've never been to New York.

WALTER. (*He enters. We feel he has relieved himself but the edge of unreality is still with him. Crosses D.L. front of table to the kitchen.*) New York ain't got nothing Chicago ain't, except a bunch of hustling people all squeezed up together — being "Eastern!" (*He turns his face into a screw of displeasure.*)

GEORGE. Oh — you've been?

WALTER. *Plenty* of times.

RUTH. (*shocked at the lie*) Walter Lee Younger!

WALTER. (*staring her down*) Plenty! (*RUTH crosses U.R. of sofa to laundry on bureau. Pause.*) What we got to drink in this house? Why don't you offer this man some refreshment? (*He crosses L., front of kitchen table to icebox. To GEORGE:*) They don't know how to entertain in this house, man. (*Gets two beers.*)

GEORGE. Thank you — I don't care for anything.

WALTER. (*caught up short by the rejection, pours himself one*) Where's Mama?

RUTH. She ain't come back yet.

WALTER. (*looking GEORGE over from head to toe, scrutinizing his carefully casual tweed sports jacket, over cashmere V-neck sweater, over soft eyelet shirt and tie, and soft slacks below, finished off with white buckskin shoes*) Why all you college boys wear them faggoty-looking white shoes? (*Crosses L. front of table.*)

RUTH. Walter Lee!

(*GEORGE ignores the remark.*)

WALTER. (*laughing*) White shoes, cold as it is.

RUTH. (*crushed*) You have to excuse him—

WALTER. (*abruptly*) No, he don't! What you always excusing me for! I'll excuse myself when I needs to be excused! (*breaks up*) They look funny as hell—bad as them black knee socks Beneatha wears out of here all the time!

RUTH. It's the college *style*.

WALTER. Style, hell, she looks like she got burnt legs or something!

RUTH. Oh, Walter—

WALTER. (*sudden thought*) How's your old man making out? I understand you all going to buy that big hotel on the Drive? (*As GEORGE nods and squirms in dismay, WALTER hauls over and straddles a chair beside him, leaning close, patting his arm, etc.*) Shrewd move. Your old man is all right, man. (*tapping his head and half winking for emphasis*) I mean he knows how to operate. I mean he thinks *big*, you know what I mean. But I think he's kind of running out of ideas now. I'd like to talk to him. (*Shifting to the arm of the sofa, he is all over GEORGE, man-to-man.*) Listen, man, I got some plans that could turn this city upside down. I mean, I think like he does. *Big*. Invest big, gamble big, hell, *lose* big if you have to, you know what I mean. It's hard to find a man on this whole Southside who understands my kind of thinking—you dig? (*He scrutinizes GEORGE again, squints his eyes and leans in confidentially.*) Me and you ought to sit down and talk sometimes, man— Man, I got me some ideas—

GEORGE. (*with disinterest*) Yeah—sometimes we'll have to do that, Walter.

WALTER. (*understanding the indifference and offended, rises, replaces chair*) Yeah—well, when you get the time, man. I know you a busy little boy.

RUTH. Walter, please—

WALTER. (*bitterly, hurt*) I know ain't nothing in this world as busy as you colored college boys with your fraternity pins and white shoes—

RUTH. (*covering her face with humiliation*) Oh, Walter Lee—

WALTER. (C.L. *of sofa*) I see y'all all the time—with the books tucked under your arms—going to your "classes"—(*British "A"—mimicking their walk too*) And for what! What the hell you learning over there? Filling up your heads—(*on his fingers*) with the sociology and the psychology—(*crosses* L. *front of table*) But they teaching you how to be a man? How to take over and run the world? They teaching you how to run a rubber plantation or a steel mill? Naw—just to talk proper and read books and wear them faggoty-looking white shoes.

GEORGE. (*looking at him with distaste, a little above it all; rises, crosses* D.R.) You're all wacked up with bitterness, man.

WALTER. (*at kitchen window, starts* R. *to GEORGE; intently, almost quietly, between the teeth, glaring at the boy*) And you—ain't you bitter, man? Ain't you just about had it yet? Don't you see no stars gleaming that you can't reach out and grab? You happy?—you contented son of a bitch—(*suddenly rushing at GEORGE who jumps up and backs off in alarm*) you happy? You got it made? Bitter? Man, I'm a volcano. Bitter? Here I am a giant —surrounded by ants! Ants who can't even understand what the giant is talking about.

RUTH. (*passionately and suddenly*) Oh, Walter— Ain't you with nobody!

WALTER. (*violently*) No! 'Cause ain't nobody with me! Not even my own mother!

RUTH. Walter, that's a terrible thing to say!

(*BENEATHA, aware of the commotion, enters dressed for the evening in a soft dress and earrings, hair natural as before.*)

GEORGE. Well—hey—(*crosses c. to BENEATHA; thoughtful, with emphasis, since this is a reversal*) You look great!

WALTER. (*looking up and seeing his sister's hair for the first time*) What's the matter with your head?

BENEATHA. (*tired of the jokes now*) I cut it off, Brother.

WALTER. (*coming close to inspect it and walking around her*) Well, I'll be damned. So that's what they mean by the African BUSH!...(*breaks up at his own joke and collapses on couch.*)

BENEATHA. Ha ha. Let's go, George.

GEORGE. (*looking at her*) You know something. I like it. It's sharp. I mean it really is. (*helps her into her wrap*)

RUTH. Yes—I think so, too. (*She starts to clutch at her hair.*)

WALTER. Oh no! You leave yours alone, baby. You might turn out to have a pin-shaped head or something!

BENEATHA. See you all later. (*Kisses RUTH.*)

RUTH. Have a nice time.

GEORGE. Thanks. Good night. (*Halfway out the door, he reopens it; to WALTER*) Good night, Prometheus. (*Shuts door as WALTER tears across the room, opens it, starts out but GEORGE is gone, slams door.*)

WALTER. (*to RUTH*) Who is Promeetheeius—? (*at*

sink with beer)

RUTH. I don't know, honey. Don't worry about it.

WALTER. (*crosses above kitchen table; in a fury, pointing after George*) See there — they get to a point where they can't insult you man to man — they got to go talk about something ain't nobody never heard of! (*crosses to sink*)

RUTH. How do you know it was an insult? (*to humor him*) Maybe Promeetheeius is a nice fellow.

WALTER. (*crosses below kitchen table*) Promeetheeius! — I bet there ain't even no such thing! I bet that simple-minded clown —

RUTH. (*rises, starts to WALTER L.*) Walter —

WALTER. (*abruptly: a warning*) Don't start!

RUTH. Start what?

WALTER. Your nagging! Where was I? Who was I with — How much money did I spend?

RUTH. (*plaintively*) Walter Lee — why don't we just try to talk about it —

WALTER. (*not listening*) I been out talking with people who understand me. People who care about the things I got on my mind.

RUTH. (*wearily*) I guess that means people like Willy Harris. (*crosses U.C., then above sofa*)

WALTER. Yes, people like Willy Harris.

RUTH. (*crosses R., back of sofa to laundry; with a sudden flash of impatience*) Why don't y'all just hurry up and go into the banking business and stop talking about it!

WALTER. (*crosses U.L. above table*) Why? — You want to know why? 'Cause we all tied up in a race of people that don't know how to do nothing but moan, pray and have babies! (*The line is too bitter even for him and he hauls chair out and around and sits down.*)

RUTH. Oh, Walter—(*softly*) Honey, why can't you stop fighting me?

WALTER. (*Without thinking*) Who's fighting you? Who even cares about you—! (*This line begins the retardation of this mood.*)

RUTH. Well—(*She waits a long time and then with resignation starts to put away the laundry.*) I guess I might as well go on to bed—(*more or less to herself*) I don't know where we lost it—but we have—(*Then to him as she crosses above sofa to C.*) I—I'm sorry about this new baby, Walter—I guess maybe I better go on and do what I started—I guess I just didn't realize how bad things was with us—(*crosses R. front of sofa*) I guess I just didn't realize—(*She picks up laundry basket and starts for R. bedroom, then stops.*) You want some hot milk?

WALTER. Hot milk?

RUTH. Yes—hot milk.

WALTER. Why hot milk?

RUTH. 'Cause after all that liquor you ought to have something hot in your stomach.

WALTER. I don't want no milk.

RUTH. You want some coffee then?

WALTER. No, I don't want no coffee. I don't want nothing hot to drink. (*almost plaintively*) Why you always trying to give me something to eat!?

RUTH (*erupting in hurt and anger*) What *else* can I give you, Walter Lee Younger? (*crosses into bedroom, flings down the basket and stands facing U.S.*)

WALTER. (*He lifts his head in a new mood which began to emerge when he asked her "Who cares about you?"*) Baby, it's been rough, ain't it? (*She hears and turns.*) I guess between two people there ain't never as much understanding as folks generally thinks there is. (*She comes to doorway.*) I mean like between me and you—(*She turns to face him.*) How we gets to the place where we scared to talk softness to each other. (*He waits, thinking hard himself.*) Why you think it got to be like that? (*He is thoughtful, almost as a child would be.*) Ruth, what is it gets into people ought to be close?

RUTH. I don't know, honey. I think about it a lot.

WALTER. On account of you and me, you mean. The way something's come down between us.

RUTH. There ain't so much between us, Walter—Not when you come to me and try to talk to me. Try to be with me—a little, even.

WALTER. Sometimes—sometimes—I don't even know how to try.

RUTH. (*crossing slowly toward him*) Walter—

WALTER. Yes—?

RUTH. (*coming to him, gently and with misgiving, but coming to him*) Honey—Life don't have to be like this. I mean sometimes people can do things so that things are better—(*She comes up behind him, stroking his head, groping for the words*) You remember how we used to talk when Travis was born—About the way we were going to live—the kind of house...(*She reaches into his shirt.*) Well, it's all starting to slip away from us....

(*He turns to look at her, puts his head against the new life in her belly, then reaches up and draws her face to his. They kiss and cling hungrily. A key is heard in the door. RUTH clings involuntarily, MAMA enters and WALTER breaks away as RUTH stands shaken in frustration.*)

WALTER. Mama, where have you been?

MAMA. (*puts hat and handbag on bureau*) My—them steps is getting longer and longer. Whew! (*She ignores*

WALTER.) How you feeling this evening, Ruth? (*She crosses L. to closet, hangs up coat, gets slippers.*)

(*RUTH shrugs, disturbed at having been prematurely interrupted and watching her husband knowingly.*)

WALTER. Mama, where have you been all day?

MAMA. (*still ignoring him and crossing to C. with slippers from closet*) Where's Travis?

RUTH. (*crosses R. to bedroom with folded clothes, exits*) I let him go out and he ain't come back yet. Boy, is he going to get it!

WALTER. Mama—!

MAMA. (*as if she has heard him for the first time*) Yes son? (*crosses, sits chair R. of kitchen table*)

WALTER. Where did you go this afternoon?

MAMA. (*putting on slippers*) I went downtown to tend to some business that I had to tend to.

WALTER. What kind of business?

MAMA. You know better than to question me like a child, Brother. (*RUTH re-enters*)

WALTER. (*bending over the table*) Where were you, Mama! (*bringing his fists down and shouting*) Mama, you didn't go do something with that money, something crazy!

(*The front door opens slowly and TRAVIS peeks his head in less than hopefully.*)

TRAVIS. (*to his mother*) Mama, I—(*WALTER, interrupted, crosses away in frustration*)

RUTH. "Mama, I," nothing! (*grabbing and shaking him, letting it all out on him*) You're going to get it, boy! Get on in that bedroom and get yourself ready!

TRAVIS. But I—

MAMA. Why don't you never let the child explain hisself?

RUTH. Keep out of it now, Lena! (*MAMA clamps her lips together and RUTH drags her son menacingly toward bedroom.*) A thousand times I have told you not to go off like that—

MAMA. Well—at least let me tell him something. I want him to be the first one to hear—Come here, baby. (*She holds out her arms and TRAVIS escapes onto his Grandmama's lap.*) Travis—(*She takes him by the shoulders and looks into his face.*) You know that money we got in the mail this morning?

TRAVIS. Yes'm—

MAMA. Well—what do you think your grandmama gone and done with that money?

(*WALTER crosses in to behind the kitchen table.*)

TRAVIS. I don't know, Grandmama.

MAMA. (*putting her finger on his nose for emphasis*) She went and she bought you a house! (*The explosion comes from WALTER as the beer glass cracks in his hand. He crosses into kitchen and, his back to them, reaches for back pocket handkerchief to wrap his hand. RUTH crosses to assist but he raises a hand in warning not to touch him. MAMA turns TRAVIS from the scene.*) You glad about the house? It's going to be yours when you get to be a man.

TRAVIS. Yes'm. I always wanted to live in a house.

MAMA. All right, gimme some sugar, then—(*TRAVIS puts his arms around her neck as she watches her son over his shoulder. Then, to TRAVIS, after the embrace:*) Now when you say your prayers tonight, you thank God and your grandfather—'cause it was him who give you the house—in his way.

RUTH. (*crosses L. to TRAVIS and MAMA; taking the*

boy from her and pushing him toward the bedroom)
Now you get out of here and get ready for your beating.

TRAVIS. Aw, Mama—Aw—gee—(*She hauls him squealing
and clinging for dear life to bedroom.*)

RUTH. Get on in there—(*closing the door behind him
and turning, radiant, to her mother-in-law*) So you went
and did it! (*at L. end of sofa*)

MAMA. (*quietly, looking at her son with pain*) Yes, I
did.

RUTH. (*raising both arms classically*) PRAISE GOD!
(*She cavorts but stops short as WALTER turns to
regard her betrayal, their eyes meet, and he turns as
swiftly away. She crosses toward him in kitchen. With
all the force that is in her: a last ditch effort to breach
the walls.*) *Please,* honey—let me be glad—you be glad,
too. Oh, Walter—a home—a home. (*She reaches out
helplessly—not quite daring to touch the raw wounds—
and at last crosses back to MAMA at table.*)
Well—where is it? How big is it? How much it going to
cost—?

MAMA. Well—

RUTH. When we moving?

MAMA. (*smiling at her*) First of the month.

RUTH. (*crosses C. above MAMA; throwing back her
head with jubilance*) PRAISE GOD!

MAMA. (*tentatively, still looking at her son's back
turned against both of them*) It's—it's a nice house, too
—(*WALTER is L. in kitchen. MAMA cannot help
speaking directly to him; she is almost like a girl now in
the imploring quality she uses to him.*) Three bedrooms—
nice big one for you and Ruth—Me and Beneatha still
have to share our room but Travis have one of his own—
and—(*with difficulty*) I figures if the—new baby—is a
boy we could get one of them double-decker outfits—

And there's a yard with a little patch of dirt where I could maybe get to grow me a few flowers — And a nice big basement —

RUTH. Walter, honey, be glad — (*crosses* L. *to WALTER front of table*)

MAMA. (*still sitting* R. *of kitchen table; still to WALTER's back, fingering things on the table*) 'Course I don't want to make it sound fancier than it is — It's just a plain little old house — but it's built good and solid and it will be *ours*. Walter Lee — it makes a difference in a man when he can walk on floors that belong to *him* —

RUTH. (*crossing in* R. *toward MAMA above table*) Where is it?

MAMA. (*frightened at this telling*) Well — well — it's out there in Clybourne Park —

(*RUTH's radiance fades abruptly and WALTER finally turns slowly to face his mother with incredulity and hostility.*)

RUTH. (*between MAMA and WALTER*) Where?

MAMA. (*too matter-of-factly*) 406 Clybourne Street, Clybourne Park.

RUTH. (*back of kitchen table*) Clybourne Park? Mama, there ain't no colored people living in Clybourne Park.

MAMA. (*a beat; almost idiotically*) Well, there's going to be some now.

WALTER. (*bitterly*) So that's the peace and comfort you went out and bought for us today!

MAMA. (*raising her eyes to meet his finally*) Son — I just tried to find the nicest place for the least amount of money for my family.

(*WALTER turns away.*)

RUTH. (*sits chair* L. *of table; trying to recover from the shock*) Well—well—'course I ain't one never been 'fraid of no crackers, mind you—but—well—wasn't there no *other* houses . . . nowhere?

MAMA. Them houses they put up for colored in them areas way out all seem to cost twice as much as other houses. I did the best I could.

RUTH. (*Who has been rather struck senseless with the news in its various degrees of goodness and trouble, sits a moment, her fists propping her chin in thought, and then she starts to rise, bringing her fists down with vigor and the radiance spreading from cheek to cheek again.*) Well—WELL!—All I can say is—if this is my time in life—*MY* TIME—to say GOOD-BYE—(*And she builds with momentum as she starts to circle the room with an exuberant, almost tearfully happy release.*) to these God-damned cracking walls!—(*She pounds the walls.*) and these marching roaches!—(*She wipes at an imaginary army of marching roaches.*) and that cramped little closet which ain't now or never was no kitchen!—then I say it loud and good, HALLELUYAH! AND GOOD-BYE, MISERY—I DON'T NEVER WANT TO SEE YOUR UGLY FACE AGAIN! (*She laughs joyously, having practically destroyed the apartment, and flings her arms up and lets them come down happily, slowly, reflectively over her abdomen, aware for the first time perhaps that the life therein pulses with happiness and not despair.*) Lena—?

MAMA. (*moved, watching her happiness*) Yes, honey—?

RUTH. (*looking off*) Is there—is there a whole lot of sunlight?

MAMA. (*simply*) Yes, child, there's a whole lot of sunlight.

(*Long pause.*)

RUTH. (*collecting herself and crossing above sofa to the bedroom where TRAVIS is*) Well—I guess I better see 'bout Travis. (*joyously*) Lord, I sure don't feel like WHIPPING nobody today! (*She exits; through the bedroom scrim we can see her advancing on, then embracing TRAVIS.*)

MAMA. (*The mother and son are left alone now and MAMA waits a long time, considering deeply, before she speaks.*) Son—you—you understand what I done, don't you? I—I just seen my family falling apart today—just falling to pieces in front of my eyes. We couldn't of gone on like we was today. We was going backwards 'stead of forwards—talking 'bout killing babies and wishing each other was dead. When it gets like that in life—you just got to do something different, push on out and do something bigger—(*She waits.*) I wish you say something, son—I wish you'd say how deep inside you think I done the right thing—

WALTER. (*turning and crossing slowly to the door and finally turning there and speaking measuredly*) What you need me to say you done right for? *You* the head of this family. You run our lives like you want to. It was your money and you did what you wanted with it. So what you need for me to say it was all right for? (*bitterly, to hurt her as deeply as he knows is possible*) So you butchered up a dream of mine—you—(*pointing at her*) who always talking 'bout your children's *dreams*—(*He starts out.*)

MAMA. Walter Lee—(*He just closes the door behind him. MAMA sits on alone thinking heavily.*)

CURTAIN

SCENE 2

TIME: *Friday night. A few weeks later.*

AT RISE: *Packing crates mark the intention of the family to move. BENEATHA and GEORGE come in, presumably from an evening out again.* Loud ad libs precede their entrance, presumably as GEORGE tries to kiss her.* "Will you stop it!" *He opens door; she slips by him, snaps on floor lamp, sits on sofa.*

GEORGE. O.K.—O.K., whatever you say—(*He sits on broken sofa spring, moves over, tries to embrace her.*)

BENEATHA. George! Please!

GEORGE. Look, we've had a nice evening; let's not spoil it, huh? (*He turns her head and tries to nuzzle in and she again turns away from him, not with distaste but momentary disinterest, in a mood to pursue what they were talking about.*)

BENEATHA. I'm trying to talk to you.

GEORGE. (*crosses U.R. of sofa*) We always talk.

BENEATHA. Yes—and I love to talk.

GEORGE. (*exasperated*) I know it and I don't mind it sometimes—Look, I want you to cut it out, see—the moody stuff. I don't like it. You're a nice-looking girl—

---

*In style and color their dress is distinctly different than in the previous scene as it must be clear to the audience that this is not the same night.

all over. That's all you need, honey, forget the atmosphere. Guys aren't going to go for the atmosphere—they're going to go for what they see. Be glad for that. Beneatha, please drop the Garbo routine. It doesn't go with you. (*He sits.*) As for myself, I want a nice—(*groping*) simple—(*thoughtfully*) sophisticated girl—Not a poet—O.K.? (*Starts to kiss her. She turns her face away. He jumps up.*)

BENEATHA. George, why are you angry?

GEORGE. Because this is stupid! I don't go out with you to discuss the nature of quiet desperation or to hear all your thoughts—because the world will go on thinking what it thinks regardless—

BENEATHA. Then why read books? Why go to school?

GEORGE. (*trying vainly, with artificial patience, to contain himself; on his fingers*) It's simple. You read books—to learn facts—to get grades—to pass the course—to get a degree. That's all—it has nothing to do with thoughts.

BENEATHA. (*a long pause*) I see. (*He starts to sit, satisfied to have made his point.*) Good night, George.

(*GEORGE jumps up, looks at her a little oddly and crosses
       U.C. to door, but MAMA, entering with a string bag of
       groceries, interrupts. He turns away.*)

MAMA. Hello, George, how are you feeling?

GEORGE. (*utterly frustrated*) Fine—fine; how are you?

MAMA. Oh, a little tired. You know them steps can get you after a day's work. You all have a nice time at the game?

GEORGE. Yes—a fine time! A fine time!

MAMA. (*Sizes up the situation, opens door. Polite but absolute dismissal.*) Well, good night, George. (*He looks at her, confounded, and exits. She closes the door.*) Hello, honey—What you sitting like that for?

BENEATHA. I'm just sitting.

MAMA. Well, now that your company's gone, why don't you make up Travis' bed? (*BENEATHA rises, gets bedclothes from U.R. armchair, starts making TRAVIS' bed.*) Didn't you have a nice time? (*She puts on light D.L.*)

BENEATHA. No.

MAMA. (*crosses D.L. above table to kitchen with string bag of groceries*) No? What's the matter?

BENEATHA. Mama, George is a fool—honest.

MAMA. (*Hustling around unloading her packages, she stops.*) Is he, baby?

BENEATHA. Yes. (*crosses R. for coat*)

MAMA. You sure?

BENEATHA. (*crosses U.C.*) Yes.

MAMA. Well—I guess you better not waste your time with no fools.

BENEATHA. (*She looks up at her mother, watching her put groceries in the icebox. Finally she gathers up her things and starts to go into the L. bedroom. At the door she stops and looks back at her mother.*) Mama—

MAMA. Yes, baby—

BENEATHA. Thank you.

MAMA. For what?

BENEATHA. For understanding me this time.

(*As she exits quickly, the phone rings. MAMA stands looking at the place where BENEATHA just stood, smiling a little perhaps. RUTH enters.*)

RUTH. Now don't you fool witn any of this stuff, *Lena—(gets the phone)* Hello—Just a minute. (*crosses to R. door*) Walter, it's Mrs. Arnold. (*waits, crosses back to phone, then tense*) Hello—Yes, this is his wife speaking—He's lying down now—Yes—well, he'll be in tomorrow. He's been very sick—(*WALTER enters and stands listening in doorway, enjoying her discomfort.*) Yes—I know we should have called, but we were so sure he'd be able to come in today—Yes—yes, I'm very sorry —Yes—Thank you very much. (*Hangs up.*) That was Mrs. Arnold.

WALTER. (*indifferently*) Was it?

RUTH. She said if you don't come in tomorrow that they are getting a new man —

WALTER. (*crosses D.R. to radio, with deliberate cutting indifference: intended to wound as he has been wounded*) Ain't that sad—ain't that crying sad?

RUTH. She said Mr. Arnold has had to take a cab for three days—Walter, you ain't been to work for three days! (*This is a revelation to her.*) Where you been, Walter Lee Younger? (*WALTER looks at her and starts to laugh.*) You're going to lose your job.

WALTER. That's right—(*sits DS. arm of chair D.R., turns on radio and listens for music.*)

RUTH. Oh, Walter, and with your mother working like a dog every day —

WALTER. That's sad, too—Everything is sad. (*A steamy deep BLUES INSTRUMENTAL comes up.*)

MAMA. What you been doing these three days, Son?

WALTER. Mama—you don't know all the things a man what got "leisure" can find to do in this city. What's this—Friday night? Well—Wednesday I borrowed Willy Harris' car and I went for a drive—just me and myself, and I drove and drove—way out—way past South

Chicago, and I parked the car and I sat and looked at the steel mills all day long. I just sat and looked at them big black chimneys for hours. Then I drove back and I went to—the Green Hat. (*Each time he says "Green Hat" he is quietly twisting the knife in MAMA.*) And Thursday —Thursday I borrowed the car again and I pointed it the other way and I drove (*MAMA sits.*) for hours—way, way up to Wisconsin, and I looked at the farms. I just drove and looked at the farms. Then I drove back and I went to the Green Hat. And today—today I didn't get the car. Today I just walked all over the Southside. And I looked at— (*familiarly, ironically*) the *Nee*groes and they looked at me, and finally I sat down on the curb at 39th and South Parkway and I just sat there and watched the *Nee*groes go by. And then I went to the Green Hat. (*RUTH goes out quietly. To her back*) Y'all sad? Y'all depressed? (*starts for closet and his coat*) And you know where I am going right now—?

MAMA. (*turning away*) Big Walter, is this the harvest of our days?

WALTER. You know what I like about the Green Hat—? (*withdrawing utterly into the bitter sweetness of the music as it pulses through him: beyond despair and rubbing her nose in it*) I like this little cat they got there who blows a sax. (*imitating*) He blows. He talks to me. He ain't but 'bout five feet tall and he's got a conked head and his eyes is always closed and he's all music—

MAMA. Walter—

WALTER. And there's another fellow who plays the piano—and they got a sound. I mean they can work on some music—They got the best little combo in the world in the Green Hat—You can just sit there and drink and listen to them three men play and you realize that don't nothing count worth a damn, but being there—

MAMA. (*rises, crosses* D.L.C.) I've helped do it to you,

haven't I, son? Walter, I been wrong.

WALTER. (*sits armchair* D.R.) Naw—you ain't never been wrong about nothing, Mama.

MAMA. (*crosses* R. *to WALTER*) Listen to me now. I say I been wrong, son. That I been doing to you what the rest of the world been doing to you. (*She turns off radio.*) Walter—(*She stops and he looks up slowly at her and she meets his eyes evenly.*) what you ain't never understood is that I ain't got nothing, don't own nothing, ain't never really wanted nothing that wasn't for you. There ain't nothing as precious to me—there ain't nothing worth holding on to, money, dreams, nothing else—if it means—if it means it's going to destroy my boy. (*Crosses* U.R.C. *to buffet for her pocketbook and money. He watches her without speaking or moving.*) I paid the man thirty-five hundred dollars down on the house. That leaves sixty-five hundred dollars. Monday morning I want you to take this money and put three thousand dollars in a savings account for Beneatha's medical schooling. (*WALTER rises, crosses* U.C.) The rest you put in a checking account—with your name on it. And from now on any penny that comes out of it or go in it is for you to look after. For you to decide. (*puts money on coffee table and drops her hands a little helplessly*) It ain't much, but it's all I got in the world and I'm putting it in your hands. I'm telling you to be the head of this family like you supposed to be. (*crosses* L., *front of table, toward her room*)

WALTER. Mama—(*She turns.*) You trust me like that, Mama?

MAMA. I ain't never stop trustin' you. Like I ain't never stop lovin' you.

(*She exits and WALTER sits looking at the money. He crosses to her room, starts to knock but doesn't, stands thinking, goes to phone, starts to dial, hangs up, crosses to son's made-up bed and smiles contemplating it, then reaches out for the money but stands, hand poised, unable to touch it. At last, with a cry of joy, he snatches it up as TRAVIS enters, for bed.*)

TRAVIS. What's the matter, Daddy? You drunk?

WALTER. (*sweetly, more sweetly than we have ever known him*) No, Daddy ain't drunk. Daddy ain't going to never be drunk again.

TRAVIS. (*unconvinced*) Well, good night, Daddy. (*draws the covers up and buries head in pillow*)

WALTER. Son, I feel like talking to you tonight

TRAVIS. About what?

WALTER. Oh, about a lot of things. (*kneels R. of sofa, facing TRAVIS*) About you and what kind of man you going to be when you grow up. . . . Son—son, what do you want to be when you grow up?

TRAVIS. A bus driver.

WALTER. (*flops over dead on floor, arms out*) A what? Man, that ain't nothing to want to be!

TRAVIS. Why not?

WALTER. 'Cause, man—it ain't big enough—you know what I mean.

TRAVIS. I don't know then. Sometimes Mama asks me that too. And when I tell her I just want to be like you, she says she don't want me to be like that. And sometimes she says she does.

WALTER. (*gathering him up in his arms*) You know what, Travis? In seven years you going to be seventeen years old. And things is going to be very different with us. And one day when you are seventeen I'll come home —home from my office—

TRAVIS. You don't work in no office, Daddy.

WALTER. No—but after tonight. After what your daddy gonna do tonight, there's going to be offices—a whole lot of offices. (*gets up*)

TRAVIS. What you gonna do tonight, Daddy?

WALTER. You wouldn't understand yet, son, but your daddy's gonna make a transaction. A business transaction that's going to change our lives. That's how come one day when you 'bout seventeen I'll come home and I'll be pretty tired, you know what I mean, after a day of conferences and secretaries getting things wrong the way they do... 'cause an executive's life is hell, man! And I'll pull the car up the driveway...just a plain black Chrysler, I think, with white walls—no—*black* tires. More elegant. Rich people don't have to be flashy... though I'll have to get something a little sportier for Ruth—maybe a Cadillac convertible to do her shopping in. And I'll come up the steps to the house and the gardener will be clipping away at the hedges and he'll say, "Good evening, Mr. Younger." And I'll say, "Hello, Jefferson, how are you this evening?" And I'll go inside and Ruth will meet me at the door and we'll kiss and she'll take my arm and we'll go upstairs to your room to see you sitting on the floor with the catalogues (*lays out magazines on coffee table like catalogues*) of all the great schools in America around you. All the great schools in the world! And—and I'll say, all right son—it's your seventeenth birthday, what is it you've decided? Just tell me where you want to go to school and you'll *go*. Just tell me, what it is you want to be—and you'll *be* it... Whatever you want to be—Yessir! (*He hold his arms open.*) You just name it, son—(*TRAVIS crosses into them and WALTER lifts him high.*) And I'll hand you the world!

(BLACKOUT)

SCENE 3

TIME: *Saturday, one week later.*

Before the curtain, RUTH's voice, a strident, dramatic church alto, cuts through the silence. It is, in the darkness, a triumphant surge, a penetrating statement of expectation: "Oh Lord, I don't feel no ways tired! Children, Oh Glory Halleluyah!"*

AT RISE: *As the curtain rises we see that RUTH is alone in the living room, packing bric-a-brac in carton on chair against US. wall. Crosses L., stands on chair L., removes ornament from L. wall, crosses R. and packs it in box above sofa. She is finishing up the family's packing. It is moving day. She is tying cartons. BENEATHA enters and watches her exuberant sister-in-law.*

RUTH. Hey!

BENEATHA. (*putting guitar case and coat in closet*) Hi.

RUTH. (*crosses* D.C. *to coffee table, pointing at a package*) Honey—look in that package there and see what I found on sale at the South Center. (*She goes to the package herself and draws out the curtains.*) Lookahere—hand-turned hems!

BENEATHA. How do you know the window size out there—?

RUTH. (*Who hadn't thought of that*) Oh—Well, they bound to fit something in the whole house. Anyhow, they was too good a bargain to pass up. (*RUTH slaps her head suddenly remembering something.*) Oh, Bennie—I meant to put a special note on that carton. That's your mama's good china.

---

*See p. 155.

BENEATHA. I'll do it. (*She finds a piece of paper and starts to draw large letters on it.*)

RUTH. (*crosses u.r. of sofa*) You know what I'm going to do soon as I get in that house?

BENEATHA. What?

RUTH. (*crosses to trunk u.l., stands on lid, removes object from above closet, crosses r., packs it*) Honey— I'm going to run me a tub of water up to here—(*with her fingers practically up to her nostrils*) and I'm going to get in it—and I am going to sit—and sit—and sit and the first person who knocks—

BENEATHA. Gets shot at sunrise!

RUTH. You said it, sister! (*noticing how large BENEATHA is absent-mindedly making the note*) Honey, they ain't going to read that from no airplane.

BENEATHA. (*laughing herself*) I guess I always think things have more emphasis if they are big, somehow.

RUTH. (*looking up at her and smiling*) You and your brother seem to have that as a philosophy of life. Lord, that man—done changed so 'round here. You know what we did last night? Me and Walter Lee?

BENEATHA. (*sitting with her coffee*) What—?

RUTH. (*smiling to herself*) We went to the movies. (*looking at BENEATHA to see if she understands*) We went to the movies. You know the last time me and Walter went to the movies together?

BENEATHA. No.

RUTH. Me, neither. That's how long it been. (*smiling again*) But we went last night. Picture wasn't much good, but that didn't matter. We went—and we held hands.

BENEATHA. Oh lord!

RUTH. We held hands—and you know what?

BENEATHA. What?

RUTH. When we come out of the show it was late and

dark and all the stores and things was closed up—and it was kind of chilly and there wasn't many people on the streets—and we was still holding hands, me and Walter.

BENEATHA. You're killing me. (*WALTER enters with a large gift-wrapped box. His happiness is deep in him, he cannot keep still with his new found exuberance. He is singing and wiggling and snapping his fingers. He puts gift in corner and puts on a record he has brought. As the music* comes up, soulful and sensuous, he dances slowly, sexily, across the room to RUTH, presents a long-stemmed rose he has been concealing, and strikes a pose inviting her to dance. She giggles at his raunchiness, embarrassed before BENEATHA, but WALTER waves that aside, and at last she melts into his arms. He dips her back low, gracefully, and dances her* D.S., *where they meld into a steaming classic body-melding "slow drag." BENEATHA regards them a long time as they dance, then drawing in her breath, with exaggeration she does not particularly mean:*) Talk about—oldddddddd—fashionedddddd—Negroes!

WALTER. (*stopping momentarily*) What kind of Negroes? (*For fun; he is not angry with her today, nor with anyone. He starts to dance with his wife again.*)

BENEATHA. Old-fashioned. (*She starts to go with the music herself and, burlesquing, dances along side them.*)

WALTER. (*to RUTH as he regards BENEATHA*) You know when all these professional *New* Negroes have their convention—(*pointing at his sister*) that is going to be the chairman of the committee on unending agitation. (*He goes on dancing, then stops.*) Race, race, race—Girl, I do believe you are the first person in the history of the entire human

---

* Excellent choice for this moment: Erskine Hawkins classic "After Hours" (RCA-Victor 447-0169).

race to successfully brain-wash your *own self!* (*BE-NEATHA breaks up and he resumes dancing with RUTH. Inspired, enjoying his tease.*) Damn, even the N DOUBLE A C P takes a holiday sometimes! (*BENEATHA and RUTH laugh.*) I can just see that chick some day looking down at some poor cat on the operating table—(*He dips and bends RUTH way back on his outstretched arm to demonstrate as the surgeon, scalpel in hand.*)—and before she starts to slice him, she'll say: (*sharpens blade like razor, then:*) Now what did you say your views on Civil Rights were—? (*He starts to slice madly, they howl and BENEATHA jumps on him. The bell sounds.*)

BENEATHA. (*crossing to the door*) Sticks and stones may break my bones but—(*She sticks out her tongue.*) words will never hurt me!

(*She opens the door and—as WALTER and RUTH kiss and cling—looks directly in the face of the stranger—a quiet-looking middle-aged white man in a business suit, hat and briefcase in hand, consulting a small piece of paper.*)

MAN. Uh—How do you do, Miss? I am looking for a Mrs.—(*He looks at the slip of paper.*) Mrs. Lena Younger—? (*He stops short, struck dumb, as RUTH giggles wildly in WALTERS arms.*)

BENEATHA. (*smoothing her hair with slight embarrassment*) Oh—yes, that's my mother. Excuse me. (*she shuts door.*) Ruth! Brother! (*Enunciating precisely but soundlessly so we can read her lips:* "There's a WHITE MAN at the door!" *They stop dancing, RUTH cuts off record, WALTER pinches her butt and she swats at him, laughing. He straightens clothes, BENEATHA opens door.*) Uh—come in please.

MAN. (*the look still on his face; recovering*) Thank you.

BENEATHA. My mother isn't here just now. Is it business?

MAN. Yes — well, of a sort.

WALTER. (*freely, the Man of the House; crosses* L. *above sofa to* L.C.) Have a seat.

(*BENEATHA crosses* D.L. *to front of table.*)

MAN. Thank you.

WALTER. I'm Mrs. Younger's son. I look after most of her business matters.

(*RUTH and BENEATHA exchange glances.*)

MAN. (*sits on broken spring of sofa, shifts uncomfortably*) Well—My name is Karl Lindner—

WALTER. (*stretching out his hand*) Walter Younger. (*LINDNER rises to shake, sits.*) This is my wife—(*LINDNER rises politely; RUTH nods, he sits.*) And my sister.

LINDNER. (*rises*) How do you do? (*starts to sit but stops mid-motion, looks behind him to make sure there is no one else to greet, and sits*)

WALTER. (*draws armchair closer, sits with RUTH on the arm beside him, arm about her. Amiably, leaning forward expectantly into the newcomer's face*) What can we do for you, Mr. Lindner!

LINDNER. (*some minor shuffling of the hat and brief case on his knees*) Well — I am a representative of the Clybourne Park Improvement Association —

WALTER. (*indicating with remark*) Why don't you sit your things on the couch?

LINDNER. Oh — yes. Thank you. (*He slides brief case and hat onto couch.*) And as I was saying — I am from the Clybourne Park Improvement Association and we have had it brought to our attention that you people—or at least your mother—has bought a piece of residential property at—(*He digs for the little slip of paper.*) 406 Clybourne Street—(*BENEATHA, eyeing it, drifts behind him.*)

WALTER. That's right. Care for something to drink? Ruth, get Mr. Lindner a beer. (*She rises.*)

LINDNER. (*upset for some reason*) Oh—no, really. I mean thank you very much, but no, thank you.

RUTH. (*innocently*) Some coffee?

LINDNER. Thank you, nothing at all. (*She sits.*) Well, I don't know how much you folks know about our organization. (*He is a gentle man; thoughtful and somewhat labored in his manner.*) It is one of these community organizations set up to look after—oh, you know things like block upkeep and special projects and we also have what we call our New Neighbors Orientation Committee—

BENEATHA. (*skeptically*) Yes—and what do they do?

LINDNER. (*turning a little to her and then returning the main force to WALTER*) Well—it's what you might call a sort of Welcoming Committee I guess. I mean they, we, I'm the chairman—go around and see the new people who move into the neighborhood and sort of give 'em the lowdown on the way we do things out in Clybourne Park.

BENEATHA. (*with false appreciation*) Uh-huh.

LINDNER. And we also have the category of what the Association calls uh—special community problems—

BENEATHA. (*caustically*) Yes—and what are some of those?

WALTER. Girl, let the man talk.

(*BENEATHA exhales heavily, crosses* L. *and above table, picks up an orange from table.*)

LINDNER. (*with understated relief*) Thank you. I would sort of like to explain this thing in my own way. I mean I want to explain in a certain way.

(*BENEATHA begins tossing the orange up and down*)

WALTER. Go ahead.

LINDNER. Yes. Well. I'm going to try to get right to the point. I'm sure we'll all appreciate that in the long run.

BENEATHA. Yes.

WALTER. Be still now!

(*BENEATHA crosses* R. *above sofa, tossing the orange in the air.*)

LINDNER. Well—

RUTH. (*innocently still*) Would you like another chair —you don't look comfortable.

LINDNER. (*more frustrated than annoyed*) No, thank you very much. Please. Well—to get right to the point I—(*A great breath and he is off at last.*) I am sure you people must be aware of some of the incidents that have happened when colored people move into certain areas—Well—because we have what I think is going to be a unique type of organization in American community life—not only do we deplore that kind of thing—but we are trying to do something about it. (*WALTER gestures approvingly and BENEATHA halts with the tossing and turns with a new and quizzical interest to LINDNER. She crosses* D.R. *of sofa to* U.L *of WALTER's chair.*) We feel—(*gaining in confidence in his mission due to the interest in the faces of the people he is talking to*) We feel that most of the trouble in this world, when you come right down to it—(*He pounds his fist just a little for emphasis on his knee.*) Most of the trouble exists because people just don't sit down and talk to each other.

RUTH. (*nodding as she might in church, pleased with the remark*) You can say that again, Mister.

LINDNER. (*also more encouraged by such affirmation*) That we don't try hard enough to understand the other fellow's problem. The other guy's point of view.

RUTH. Now that's right. (*WALTER gestures that LINDNER is right on target.*)

LINDNER. Yes — and that's why I was elected to come here this afternoon and talk to you people and see if we couldn't find some way to work this thing out. Anybody can see that you are a nice family of folks, hard working and honest, I'm sure. Today everybody knows what it means to be an outsider. [And of course there is always somebody who is out to take advantage of people who don't understand.

WALTER. What do you mean?

LINDNER.] Well — you see our community is made up of people who've worked hard as the dickens for years to build up that little community. We're not rich and fancy people; just hard-working honest people who don't really have much but those little homes and a dream of the kind of community we want to raise our children in. Now I don't say we are perfect and there is a lot wrong in some of the things we want. But you've got to admit that a man, right or wrong, has the right to want to have the neighborhood he lives in a certain kind of way. And at the moment the overwhelming majority of our people out there feel that people get along better;

take more of a common interest in the life of the community when they share a common background. (*As they react, he rushes to reassure them.*) Now I want you to believe me when I tell you that race prejudice simply doesn't enter into it. It is a matter of the people of Clybourne Park believing, rightly or wrongly, as I say, that for the happiness of all concerned that our Negro families are happier when they live in their *own* communities.

BENEATHA. (*with a grand and bitter gesture*) This, friends, is the Welcoming Committee!

WALTER. (*dumbfounded*) Is this what you came marching all the way over here to tell us?

LINDNER. Well now we've been have a fine conversation I hope you'll hear me all the way through.

WALTER. (*tightly*) Go ahead, man.

LINDNER. You see — in the face of all the things I have said, we are prepared to make your family a very generous offer —

BENEATHA. Thirty pieces and not a coin less!

WALTER. Yeah — ?

LINDNER. (*putting on his glasses and drawing out a form from the brief case*) Our association is prepared through the collective effort of our people to buy the house from you at a financial gain to your family.

RUTH. (*rises, crosses L. front of table*) Lord have mercy, ain't this the living gall!

WALTER. All right, you through? (*Rises.*)

LINDNER. Well, I want to give you the exact terms of the arrangement —

WALTER. We don't want to hear no exact terms of no arrangements. I want to know if you got any more to tell 'bout getting together.

LINDNER. (*taking off his glasses*) Well — I don't suppose that you feel —

WALTER. Never mind how I feel — you got any more to say 'bout how people ought to sit down and talk to each other? (*He strides to the door and opens it wide.*) Get out of my house, man.

LINDNER. (*looking around at the hostile faces and reaching and assembling his hat and brief case; crosses* L. *to* U.C.) I don't understand why you people are reacting this way. What do you think you are going to gain by moving where you—aren't wanted and where some elements—well—people can get awful worked up when they feel that their whole way of life and everything they've ever worked for is threatened—

WALTER. (*Restraining himself: quietly, unable even to look at the man*) Get out.

LINDNER. (*at the door, holding a small card*) Well, I'm sorry it went like this.

WALTER. (*Facing him*) Get out!

LINDNER. (*from the door with deep passion:*) You just can't force people to change their hearts, son. (*He turns and puts his card on buffet and exits.*)

(*WALTER pushes the door to with stinging hatred; he picks up and looks at the card, puts it down. RUTH sits grimly* L. *of kitchen table, BENEATHA on arm of chair* D.R. *They say nothing for several seconds. MAMA and TRAVIS enter* C. *door. TRAVIS goes into bedroom* R. *with boxes.*)

MAMA. (*puts hat, bag, stringbag and broom on crate back of sofa; crosses* D.L., *front of table, putting sticks and string on table; gets plant from window; crosses* R. *above table; sits*) Well—this all the packing got done since I left out of here this morning? I testify before God that my children got all the energy of the *dead!* What time the moving men due—?

BENEATHA. Four o'clock. You had a caller, Mama. (*She is smiling, teasingly. She crosses* L. *front of sofa to MAMA.*)

MAMA. Sure enough—who?

BENEATHA. (*her arms folded saucily*) The Welcoming Committee.

(*WALTER smothers laugh and RUTH rolls eyes.*)

MAMA. (*innocently*) Who?

BENEATHA. The Welcoming Committee. They said they're sure going to be glad to see you when you get there.

WALTER. (*devilishly*) Yeah, they said they can't hardly wait to see your face. (*laughter*)

(*BENEATHA crosses* R. *above sofa.*)

MAMA. (*sensing their facetiousness and looking up and putting her hands on her hips*) What's the matter with you all?

WALTER. Ain't nothing the matter with us. We just telling you 'bout the gentleman who came to see you. From the (*mimicking LINDNER*) Clybourne Park Improvement Association. (*They break up.*)

MAMA. What he want?

RUTH. To welcome you, honey.

WALTER. He said—He said if it's one thing they don't have that they just DYING to have out there and that's a fine family of fine colored people!

RUTH. Yeah! He left his card—

BENEATHA. (*taking card from table and handing to MAMA*) In case.

MAMA. (*throws it on the floor—understanding and looking off as she draws up her chair to the table where she has put her plant and some sticks and some cord. WALTER sprawls on sofa.*) Father, give us strength. (*knowingly and without fun*) Did he threaten us?

BENEATHA. Oh, Mama—they don't do it like that any more. He talked Brotherhood. He said everybody ought to learn how to sit down and hate each other with good Christian fellowship. (*She and WALTER slap hands.*)

MAMA. (*sadly*) Lord, protect us—

RUTH. (*still in chair L. of kitchen table*) You should hear the money those folks raised to buy the house back. All we paid and then some.

BENEATHA. (*crosses L. to above table*) What they think we going to do—eat 'em?

RUTH. No, honey, marry 'em.

MAMA. (*shaking her head*) Lord, Lord, Lord—

RUTH. (*rises, takes wrapped bowl of fruit to barrel*) Well—that's the way the crackers crumble. (*As they turn to stare at her:*) Joke.

BENEATHA. (*laughingly, noticing what her mother is doing*) Mama, what are you doing?

MAMA. Fixing my plant so it won't get hurt none on the way—

BENEATHA. Mama, you going to take *that* to the new house?

MAMA. Uh huh—

BENEATHA. That raggedy-looking old thing?!

MAMA. (*rises, looking at her; enunciating grandly*) It— expresses *ME*!

(*WALTER and RUTH howl and BENEATHA too is amused.*)

RUTH. (*with delight, to BENEATHA*) So there! Miss Thing!

(*WALTER suddenly rises, crosses* U.R. *above sofa, crosses* L. *to MAMA and bends down behind her and squeezes her in his arms with all his strength. She is overwhelmed by the suddeness of it and her manner is like that of RUTH with TRAVIS.*)

MAMA. Look out now, boy! You make me mess up my thing here!

WALTER. (*His face lit, he slips down on his knees beside her, his arms still about her.*) Mama — you know what it means to climb up in the chariot?

MAMA. (*gruffly, very happy*) Get on away from me now —

RUTH. (*near the gift-wrapped package, trying to catch WALTER's eye*) Psst —

WALTER. What the old song say, Mama — ?

RUTH. Walter — Now? (*She is pointing at the package.*)

(*TRAVIS enters* R. *with box and hockey stick which he puts on bureau.*)

WALTER. (*sweetly, singing playfully in MAMA's face*) "I got wings — You got wings — All God's children got wings —"

MAMA. Boy — get out of my face and do some work —

WALTER. "When I get to heaven gonna put on them wings. I'm gonna fly all over God's heaven —" (*RUTH gets the package*)

BENEATHA. (*teasingly from across the room*) Everybody talking 'bout heaven ain't going there!

WALTER. (*as RUTH approaches with package teasingly "concealed" behind her*) I don't know. You think we ought to give her this—Seems to me she ain't been very co-operative around here.

(*TRAVIS crosses L. to above table.*)

MAMA. (*eyeing the box which is obviously a gift*) What is it?

WALTER. Well-what y'all think? Should we give it to her?

RUTH. (*Keeping the package just out of reach*) Oh—she was pretty good today.

MAMA. I'll good you—(*She turns her eyes to the box again. RUTH hands it to her and the family surrounds her.*

(*TRAVIS crosses down and stands in front of the table between MAMA's chair on the R. and BENEATHA on the L.*)

BENEATHA. Open it, Mama.

(*MAMA stands up, looks at it—turns and looks at all of them and then presses her hands together and does not open it.*)

WALTER. (*placing the package on the chair; sweetly*) Open it, Mama. It's for you. (*MAMA looks in his eyes—it is the first present without Christmas in her life. Slowly she opens her package and lifts out, one by one, a brand new sparkling set of gardening tools. Prodding.*) Read the note, Mama. Ruth wrote the note.

MAMA. (*picking up the card and adjusting her*

glasses) "To our own Mrs. Miniver — Love from Brother, Ruth and Beneatha." Ain't that lovely. Thank you, son.

TRAVIS. (*crosses to* C. *tugging at his father's sleeve*) Daddy, can I give her mine now?

WALTER. All right, son.

(*TRAVIS flies to bedroom* R.)

MAMA. (*clutching the tools*) Now I don't have to use my knives and forks no more!

WALTER. Travis didn't want to go in with the rest of us, Mama. He got his own. (*somewhat amused*) We don't know what it is —

TRAVIS. (*racing back into the room with a large hat-box, crossing* D.R. *front of sofa and putting it in front of his grandmother*) Here!

MAMA. Lord have mercy, Baby. You done brought your grandmother a hat?

TRAVIS. (*very proud*) Open it!

(*MAMA does, and stares into the box in semi-shock as WALTER covers mouth and walks away to conceal laughter. MAMA lifts out an elaborate, wide, artificial fruit-covered gardening hat and all adults break up at the sight of it.*)

RUTH. Travis, honey, what is that?

TRAVIS. (*who thinks it is beautiful and appropriate*) It's a gardening hat! Like the ladies always have on in the magazines when they work in their gardens.

BENEATHA. (*giggling fiercly*) Travis — we were trying to make Mama "Mrs. Miniver" — not Scarlet O'Hara!

MAMA. (*indignantly*) What's the matter with y'all! This here is a beautiful hat! (*absurdly*) I always wanted me one just like it! (*She pops it on her head to prove it to her grandson and it is as ludicrous as everything and considerably oversize and everyone but TRAVIS breaks up.*)

RUTH. Hot dog! Go, Mama!

WALTER. (*doubled up with laughter*) I'm sorry, Mama—but you look like you ready to go out and chop you some cotton, sure enough!

(*All laugh except MAMA, out of deference to TRAVIS' feelings.*)

MAMA. (*gathering TRAVIS up to her*) Bless your heart—this is the prettiest hat I ever owned! (*RUTH and BENEATHA chime in congratulations to TRAVIS noisily and insincerely, but WALTER comes to the rescue, plucking him from the midst of the women and raising him high as he crosses away, then hugs him, man-to-man.*) What we all standing around here for? We ain't finished packin' yet. Bennie, you ain't packed one book.

(*The doorbell rings.*)

BENEATHA. That couldn't be the movers—it's not hardly two good yet—

(*She goes L. into her room. MAMA starts for the C. door.*)

WALTER. (*turning, stiffening*) Wait—wait—I'll get it. (*He stands and looks at the door.*)

MAMA. You expecting company, son?

WALTER. (*just looking at the door*) Yeah—yeah—

(*MAMA looks at RUTH and they exchange innocent and unfrightened glances.*)

MAMA. Travis—you run to the hardware and get me some string cord.

(*MAMA goes out to* L. *bedroom. WALTER turns and looks at RUTH. TRAVIS goes to dish for money.*)

RUTH. Why don't you answer the door, man?

WALTER. (*suddenly bounding across the floor to her*) 'Cause sometimes it hard to let the future begin! (*stooping down in her face*) "I got wings! You got wings!" (*The doorbell rings a second time.*) "When I get to heaven—" (*He crosses to the door and throws it open. TRAVIS exits; and there stands a very slight little man in a thread bare business suit and with hat pulled down tightly, brim up, around his forehead. WALTER leans deep in face, still in his jubilance. The little man just stares at him.*) "—gonna put on my wings—" (*Suddenly he stops singing and looks past the little man into the empty hallway.*) Where's Willy, man?

BOBO. He ain't with me.

WALTER. (*not disturbed, gives him some "skin"*) Oh—come on in. You know my wife.

BOBO. (*dumbly*) Yes—h'you, Miss Ruth. (*crosses* D.C.)

RUTH. (*quietly, a mood apart from her husband already, seeing BOBO*) Hello, Bobo.

WALTER. You right on time today—right on time. That's the way! (*He boxes playfully with BOBO.*) Sit down —lemme hear.

(*RUTH at* D.L. *corner of kitchen table stands stiffly, quietly as though somehow she senses death, her eyes fixed on her husband.*)

BOBO (*His frightened eyes belying his smile,* * *his hat in his hands,*) Could I please get a drink of water, before I tell you about it, Walter Lee?

(*WALTER does not take his eyes off BOBO. RUTH goes blindly to the tap and gets a glass of water and brings it dumbly to BOBO.*)

WALTER. There ain't nothing wrong, is there—

BOBO. Lemme tell you—Walter Lee. (*drains glass to the last drop as WALTER watches impatiently and at last takes it from him*) You know how it was. I got to tell you how it was. I mean first I got to tell you how it was all the way—I mean about the money I put in, Walter Lee—

WALTER. (*drawing him away* D.C. *with taut agitation now.*) What about the money you put in?

BOBO. Well—it wasn't much as we told you—me and Willy—(*He stops.*) I'm sorry, Walter. I got a bad feeling about it. I got a real bad feeling about it—

WALTER. Man, what you telling me all this for—Tell me what happened in Springfield—

BOBO. Springfield.

RUTH. (*like a dead woman*) What was supposed to happen in Springfield?

BOBO. (*to her*) This deal that me and Walter went into with Willy—Me and Willy was going to go down to Springfield and spread some money round so's we wouldn't have to wait so long for the liquor license—I mean everybody said that was the way you had to do, you understand, Miss Ruth?

---

* BOBO is not a con-man but a victim; it is an act of great courage that has brought him here.

WALTER. Man—what happened down there?

BOBO. (*a pitiful man, near tears*) I'm trying to tell you, Walter.

WALTER. (*grabs BOBO, swings him to* C. *facing* L., *screaming at him suddenly*) THEN TELL ME, GOD-DAMNIT—WHAT'S THE MATTER WITH YOU?

BOBO. Man—I didn't go to no Springfield, yesterday.

WALTER. (*halted, life hanging in the moment*) Why not?

BOBO. (*the long way, the hard way to tell*) 'Cause I didn't have no reasons to—

WALTER. Man, what are you talking about!

BOBO. (*WALTER backs him across* D.R. *front of sofa.*) I'm talking about the fact that when I got to the train station yesterday morning—eight o'clock like we planned—Man—*Willy didn't never show up.*

WALTER. Why—where was he—where is he?

BOBO. That's what I'm trying to tell you—I don't know. I waited six hours—I called his house—and I waited—six hours—I waited in that train station six hour—(*breaking into tears, looking up at WALTER with tears running down his face*) Man, *Willy is gone.*

WALTER. Gone, what you mean Willy is gone? Gone where? You mean he went by himself. Yeah, sure—(*He turns and looks anxiously at RUTH and paces* L. *around kitchen table then* R. *back to BOBO.*) maybe he didn't want too many people in on the business down there. (*looks at RUTH again, as before*) You know Willy got his own ways. (*looks back to BOBO*) Maybe you was late yesterday and he just went on down there without you. (*pacing*) Maybe—maybe—he's callin' you at home right now. Maybe—maybe—he just got sick. He's somewhere—he's got to be somewhere. We just got to find him—(*grabs*

BOBO desperately as if to lead him out) WE GOT TO!

BOBO. *(breaking free)* What's the matter with you, Walter! *When a cat take off with your money he don't leave you no road maps!*

WALTER. *(As it registers, he turns blindly; BOBO grabs and hugs him, but WALTER slips through his arms to the floor)* NO, WILLY! ...WILLY, DON'T DO IT! ... PLEASE DON'T DO IT...MAN, NOT WITH THAT MONEY! MAN, PLEASE, NOT WITH THAT MONEY...OH, GOD—DON'T LET IT BE TRUE—*(He starts to pound the floor with his fists, sobbing wildly, as RUTH turns away in horror. MAMA opens the bedroom door and enters with BENEATHA behind her.)* MAN—I TRUS-TED YOU! ...MAN, I PUT MY LIFE IN YOUR HANDS! ...MAN—THAT MONEY IS MADE OUT OF MY FATHER'S *FLESH*—!

BOBO. *(standing over him helplessly)* I'm sorry, Walter—I had my life staked on this deal, too—*(At a sign from MAMA he exits.)*

MAMA. *(to WALTER)* Son—*(She goes* D.C. *to him, bends down to him, talks quietly to his bent head.)* Son—Is it gone? Son, I gave you sixty-five hundred dollars. Is it gone? All of it? Beneatha's money, too?

WALTER. *(lifting his head slowly)* Mama—I never—went to the bank at all—

MAMA. *(still quietly, not wanting to believe it)* You mean your sister's school money—you used that too?

WALTER. Yes, all of it—it's all gone—

MAMA. *(stops and looks at both of her children and rises slowly and wanders vaguely, aimlessly away from them*)* I seen—him—night after night—come in—and look at that rug—and then look at me—the red showing in his eyes—the veins moving in his head—I seen him grow thin and old before he was forty—working and working and working like somebody's old horse — killing himself! And you—YOU GIVE IT ALL AWAY IN ONE DAY—!(*She raises her arms to strike him.*)

BENEATHA. Mama—

MAMA. Oh, God—(*She looks up to Him.*) look down here—and show me the strength.

BENEATHA. Mama—

MAMA. Father—strength—

BENEATHA. (*plaintively*) Mama—

MAMA. Strength!

CURTAIN

*NOTE: From this point foward it is very important that WALTER not sob audibly, move about or otherwise distract from, muddy or make maudlin the final moments of this scene.

ACT THREE

TIME: *An hour later.*

AT RISE: *There is a sullen light of gloom in the living room, grey light not unlike that which began the first scene of ACT I. At* R. *we can see WALTER through scrim in his room, alone with himself. He is stretched out on the bed, his shirt open, arms under his head. He does not smoke; he does not cry out; he merely lies there, looking up at the ceiling, much as if he were alone in the world. In the living room BENEATHA sits at the kitchen table still surrounded by the now almost ominous packing crates. She sits looking off. We feel that this is a mood struck perhaps an hour before, and it lingers now, full of the empty sound of profound disappointment. We see on a line from her brother's bedroom the sameness of their attitudes. Presently the doorbell rings and BENEATHA rises without ambition or interest to answer. It is ASAGAI, smiling broadly, striding into the room with energy and happy expectation and conversation.*

ASAGAI. (*crosses* R. *above sofa,* D.R., *crosses* L. *front of sofa to barrel, crosses* R. *to BENEATHA*) I came over — I thought I might help with the packing. Ah, I like the look of packing crates! A household in prepara-

tion for a journey! It depresses some people—
but for me—it is another feeling. Something full of the
flow of life, do you understand? Movement, progress—
it makes me think of Africa.

BENEATHA. Africa!

ASAGAI. What kind of mood is this? Have I told you
how deeply you move me?

BENEATHA. He gave away the money, Asagai—

ASAGAI. Who gave away what money?

BENEATHA. The insurance money. My brother gave it
away.

ASAGAI. Gave it away?

BENEATHA. He made an investment! With a man even
Travis wouldn't have trusted!

ASAGAI. And it's gone?

BENEATHA. (*sits on sofa*) Gone!

ASAGAI. (*sits next to BENEATHA on sofa.
BENEATHA rises, crosses* U.R. *of sofa, sits* R. *arm of
sofa.*) I'm very sorry—And you now?

BENEATHA. Me?—Me? Me, I'm nothing—Me. When
I was very small—we used to take our sleds out in the
winter time and the only hills we had were some ice
covered stone steps down the street. And we used to fill
them with snow and make them smooth and slide down
them all day—and it was very dangerous, you know—
far too steep—and sure enough one day a kid named
Rufus came down too fast and hit the sidewalk—and his
face just split open right there in front of us—And I
remember standing there looking at his bloody open
face thinking that was the end of Rufus. But the am-
bulance came and they took him to the hospital and they
fixed the broken bones and they sewed it all up—and the
next time I saw Rufus he just had a little line down the
middle of his face—I never got over that—

ASAGAI. What?

BENEATHA. That that was what one human being could do for another, fix him up—sew up the problem, make him all right again. That was the most marvelous thing in the world—I wanted to do that. I always thought it was the one concrete thing in the world that a human being could do. Fix up the sick, you know—and make them whole again. This was truly being God—

ASAGAI. You wanted to be God—?

BENEATHA. No—I wanted to cure. It used to be so important to me. I wanted to cure. I used to care. I mean about people and how their bodies hurt—

ASAGAI. And you've stopped caring—?

BENEATHA. Yes—I think so.

ASAGAI. (*rises*) Why?

BENEATHA. (*passionately*) Because it doesn't seem deep enough, close enough to what ails mankind! It was a child's way of seeing things—or an idealist's.

ASAGAI. Children see things very well sometimes—and idealists even better.

BENEATHA. I know that's what you think. Because you are still where I left off. You still care. You with all your talk and dreams about Africa! You still think you can patch up the world. Cure the Great Sore of Colonialism—(*loftily, mocking it*) with the "penicillin of Independence!"

ASAGAI. Yes!

BENEATHA. Independence *and then what?* What about all the crooks and thieves and just plain idiots who will come into power to steal and plunder the same as before, only now they will be black and do it in the name of the new independence—WHAT ABOUT THEM?!

ASAGAI. That will be the problem for another time. First we must get there.

BENEATHA. And where does it end?

ASAGAI. End? Who ever spoke of an end? To life? To living?

BENEATHA. An end to misery! To stupidity! Don't you see there isn't any real progress, Asagai, there is only one large circle that we march in, around and around, each of us with our own little picture in front of us — our own little mirage that we think is the future.

ASAGAI. That is the mistake.

BENEATHA. What?

ASAGAI. What you just said — about the circle. It isn't a circle. (*His gestures paint the picture as he talks.*) It is simply a long line — as in geometry, you know — one that *curves* into infinity. And because we cannot see the end, we also cannot see how it — changes. And it is very odd, but those who *see* the changes—who dream, who will not give up—are called idealists. . .and those who see *only* the circle —(*ironically*) they call each other the "realists"!

BENEATHA. Asagai, while I was sleeping in that bed in there, people went out and took the future right out of my hands! Nobody asked me—they just went out and changed my life!

ASAGAI. Was it your money?

BENEATHA. What?

ASAGAI. Was it your money he gave away?

BENEATHA. It belonged to all of us.

ASAGAI. But did you earn it? Would you have had it at all if your father had not died?

BENEATHA. No.

ASAGAI. Then isn't there something wrong in a house—in a world—where all dreams, good or bad, must depend on the death of a man? I never thought to see *you* like this, Alaiyo. *You.* Your brother made a mistake and you are grateful to him so that now you can give up the ailing human race on

account of it! You talk about what good is struggle, what
good is anything! Where are we all going and why are we
bothering!

BENEATHA. AND YOU CANNOT ANSWER IT!

ASAGAI. (*Shouting over her.*) I LIVE THE AN-
SWER! (*Long pause as he crosses to her and marshalls
the words to truly reach her.*) In my village at home it is
the exceptional man who can even read a newspaper — or who ever *sees* a book at all. (*crosses R. in to
her*) I will go home and much of what I will have to say
will seem strange to the people of my village — But I will
teach and work and things will happen, slowly and
swiftly. At times it will seem that nothing changes at
all — and then again — the sudden dramatic events which
make history leap into the future. And then quiet again.
Retrogression, even. Guns, murder, revolution. And I
even will have moments when I wonder if the quiet was
not better than all that death and hatred. But I will look
about my village at the illiteracy and disease and ignorance and I will not wonder long. And perhaps —
perhaps I will be a great man—(*She looks at him oddly,
turns away.*)I mean perhaps I will hold onto the substance
of truth—and perhaps for it I will be butchered in my bed
some night by the servants of empire—

BENEATHA. THE MARTYR!

ASAGAI. (*He smiles, softening.*) Or perhaps I shall
live to be a very old man, respected and esteemed in my
new nation — And perhaps I shall hold office and this is
what I'm trying to tell you, Alaiyo, perhaps the things I
believe now for my country will be wrong and out-
moded, and I will do terrible things to have things my
way or merely to keep my power. Don't you see there
will be young men and women, not British soldiers, but
my own black countrymen — to step out of the shadows

some night and slit my then useless throat? Don't you see, they have always been there — that they always will be? And that such a thing as my own death will be an advance — actually replenishing all that I *was.*

BENEATHA. Oh, Asagai, I know all that. (*crosses away*)

ASAGAI. Good! Then stop moaning and groaning and tell me what you plan to do.

BENEATHA. (*turning*) Do?

ASAGAI. I have a bit of a suggestion.

BENEATHA. What?

ASAGAI. (*rather quietly for him*) That when it is all over — that you come home with me —

BENEATHA. (*slapping herself on the forehead with exasperation and crossing away*) Oh — Asagai — at this moment you decide to be romantic!

ASAGAI. (*quickly understanding the misunderstanding and crossing after her*) My dear, young creature of the New World — I do not mean across the city — I mean across the ocean: home — to Africa.

BENEATHA. (*slowly understanding and turning to him with murmured amazement*) [To Africa?

ASAGAI. Yes! (*Smiling and lifting his arms playfully.*) Three hundred years later the African Prince rose up out of the seas and swept the maiden back across the middle passage over which her ancestors had come —

BENEATHA. (*unable to play*)] To — to Nigeria — ?

ASAGAI. Nigeria. Home. (*Drawing close beside her and guiding her eyes upward and out, he raises one hand to reveal the vista that awaits them. With genuine romantic flippancy:*) I will show you our mountains and our stars; and give you cool drinks from gourds and teach you the old songs and the ways of our people —

and in time—we will pretend that—(*very softly*) you have only been away for a day. Say that you'll come. (*He turns her around and takes her full in his arms in a kiss which proceeds to passion.*)

BENEATHA. (*pulling away suddenly*) You're getting me all mixed up—

ASAGAI. Why—?

BENEATHA. Too many things—too much has happened today. I don't know what I feel about anything. I'm just going to sit down and think. (*crosses* D.C., *sits on sofa and props her head on her hand*)

ASAGAI. All right, I shall leave you. (*Crosses to* C. *above table. BENEATHA starts to rise.*) No—don't get up. Just sit a while and think—Never be afraid to sit a while and think. (*goes to the* C. *door and turns*) How often I have looked at you and said, "Ah—so this is what the New World hath finally wrought—" (*He exits.*)

(*BENEATHA sits on alone. Presently WALTER enters from his room and starts to rummage through things, feverishly looking for something. She looks up and turns in her seat.*)

BENEATHA. (*hissingly, punctuating each word*) Yes—just look at what the "New World Hath Wrought!" Just look! (*She gestures with bitter disgust. Business of WALTER searching for LINDNER's card.*) There he is! *Monsieur le petit bourgeois noir* himself! There he is—Symbol of a Rising Class! Entrepreneur! Titan of the system! (*WALTER ignores her completely and picks up his coat from chair* D.R., *frantically looking and hurling things to the floor and tearing things out*

of their place in his search. BENEATHA ignores the eccentricity of his actions and goes on with the monologue of insult. Rises, crosses U.C., *attacks him back of sofa.*)
Did you dream of yachts on Lake Michigan, Brother!
Did you see yourself on that Great Day sitting down at
the Conference—(*WALTER finds it back of sofa by crate. Pushes it in his pocket and puts on his coat and rushes out without ever having looked at her. As he exits, she shouts after him the end of the following speech:*) table, surrounded by all the mighty baldheaded men in America? All halted, waiting, breathless, for your pronouncements on industry? Waiting for you—
Chairman of the Board!

(*WALTER slams the door. RUTH comes out quickly from MAMA's room* L.)

RUTH. Who was that?
BENEATHA. Your husband. (*crosses* R. *above sofa*)
RUTH. Where did he go—?
BENEATHA. (*crosses* D.R.) How do I know—Maybe
he had an appointment at U.S. Steel. (*sits on sofa*)
RUTH. (*anxiously, with frightened eyes*) You didn't
say nothing bad to him, did you?
BENEATHA. (*incredulous*) Bad—? To him? No—I told
him he was a sweet boy and full of dreams and everything is strictly peachy keen!

(*RUTH crosses to closet for her coat to go after WALTER, pauses as MAMA enters* L. *from her bedroom. MAMA is lost, vague, trying to catch hold —to make some sense of her former command of the world, but it still eludes her. A sense of waste overwhelms her gait; a measure of apology rides on her shoulders.*)

MAMA. (*goes to her plant which has remained on the table, looks at it; picks it up and takes it to the window sill and sets it outside and stands and looks at it a long moment. Then she closes the window, straightens her body with effort and turns around to her children.*) Well—ain't it a mess in here, though? (*RUTH crosses D.L. to icebox. MAMA starts unpacking barrel R. of sink. A false cheerfulness, a beginning of something.*) I guess we all better stop moping around and get some work done. All this unpacking and everything we got to do. (*RUTH raises her head slowly in response to the sense of the line; and BENEATHA in similar manner turns very slowly to look at her mother.*) One of you all better call the moving people and tell 'em not to come.

RUTH. Tell 'em not to come? (*crosses to MAMA*)

MAMA. Of course, baby. Ain't no need in 'em coming all the way here and having to go back. They charges for that, too.

RUTH. Lena, no! We gotta go. Bennie—Bennie—tell her—(*She crosses to BENEATHA.*) Tell her we can still move. The notes ain't but a hundred and twenty-five a month. (*She begins frantically to pack things.*) We got four grown people in this house—we can work—

MAMA. This just ain't our time to be trying to take on something like that.

RUTH. (*Turning and going to MAMA fast—the words pouring out with urgency and desperation as she summons up all the strength that is in her: at this moment when all has collapsed, when Beneatha and Walter and even Mama have given up, she will not let go:*) Lena—I'll work! I'll work twenty hours a day in all the kitchens in Chicago! I'll strap my baby on my back if I have to—and scrub all the floors in America and wash all the sheets in America if I have to—but we got to MOVE! We got to get OUT OF HERE!! (*She is near hysteria, out of words but eyes still pleading helplessly as she gropes to continue, knowing even as she does that she has lost. Mama reaches out to comfort her and RUTH turns sobbing into her arms.*)

MAMA. (*bravely, a stab at the old assurance*) No—I sees things differently now. Been thinking 'bout how we could fix this place up some. I seen a second hand bureau over on Maxwell Street just the other day—fit right there. (*She points to back of the sofa and RUTH wanders away from her.*) And—we can put up them new curtains in the kitchen—(*to RUTH*) And some nice screens in your room round the baby's bassinet—Why this place be looking fine. Cheer us all up so that we forget trouble ever come—(*She looks at them both, pleadingly, without conviction, sits.*) Sometimes you just got to know when to give up some things—and hold on to what you got.

(*WALTER enters from the outside looking spent and leaning against the door with coat hanging from him. At the sight of him BENEATHA turns away, and RUTH, too, can scarcely bear to look at him. But if WALTER reacts, he conceals it beneath a facade of coolly defiant, almost jaunty bravado. He has made a decision, rationalized a course of action for himself because he has HAD to. He believes a man must be tough, "realistic." And precisely because he is uneasy with it—is in fact churning within—he must press on, permit no doubt from within or response from without to come between* *him and his purpose.**)

MAMA. Where you been, son?

WALTER. (*with forced nonchalance*) Made a call.

MAMA. To who, son?

WALTER. To The Man.

MAMA. What man, baby?

WALTER. The Man, Mama. Don't you know who The Man is?

RUTH. Walter Lee?

WALTER. THE MAN. Like the guys in the streets say—The Man. Captain Boss—Mistuh Charley—Old Cap'n Please Mr. Bossman.

BENEATHA. (*suddenly*) Lindner!

WALTER. That's right. That's good. I told him to come right over.

BENEATHA. (*fiercely, understanding*) For what? What do you want to see him for!

WALTER. (*looking at his sister*) We going to do business with him.

MAMA. What you talking 'bout, son?

WALTER. Talking 'bout life, Mama. You all always telling me to see life like it is. Well—I laid in there on my back today—and I figured it out. Life just like it is. Who gets and who don't get. (*He sits down in his coat and laughs.*) Mama, you know it's all divided up. Life is. Sure enough. Between the takers and the "tooken." (*He laughs.*) Yeah. And some of us always getting "tooken." (*He laughs.*) People like Willy Harris, they don't never get "tooken." And you know why the rest of us do? 'Cause we all mixed up. Mixed up bad. We get to looking round for the right and the wrong; and we worry about it and cry about it and stay up nights trying

---

*At some point later on in this scene, in one particularly telling production, Walter began, as he talked and argued, to frantically clear the table, crumple and throw out newspapers and packaging stuffing, set beer cans in place for his meeting with Lindner.

to figure out 'bout the wrong and the right of things all the time—And all the time, man, them takers is out there operating, just taking and taking. Willy Harris? Shoot—Willy Harris don't even count. He don't even count in the big scheme of things. But I'll say one thing for old Willy—he's taught me something: to keep my eye on what does count in this world. Yeah. (*shouting out a little*) Thanks, Willy! (*crosses* R. *above sofa to door* R.)

RUTH. (*step* C.) What did you call that man for, Walter Lee?

WALTER. (*crosses* L. *to* C.) Called him to come on over to the show. Gonna put on a show for the Man. Just what he wants to see. You see, Mama? The man came here today *himself* to tell us that them people out there where you want us to move—well, they so upset they willing to pay us *not* to move! (*He laughs again.*) And—and oh, Mama—you would of been so proud of me and Ruth and Bennie—we told him to get out! Lord have mercy, we told the man to get out! Oh, we was some proud folks this afternoon, yeah. (*crosses* D.L. *above table to icebox*) We were full of that old-time stuff—

RUTH. (*crossing fiercely* D.L. *to him at icebox*) You talking 'bout taking them people's money to keep us from moving in our house?

WALTER. (*jaw-to-jaw—riding over her*) I ain't just talking 'bout it, baby—I'm telling you that's what's going to happen!

BENEATHA. Oh God! Where is the bottom! Where is the honest-to-God bottom so he can't go any farther! (*She crosses away* D.R.)

WALTER. (*crosses* R. *above table to above sofa*) Where is the bottom? Where is the bottom! You and that boy that was here today. You all want everybody to carry a flag and a spear and sing some marching songs, huh? You wanna spend your life looking into things and trying to find the right and the wrong part, huh? Yeah. You know what's going to happen to that boy some day — he'll find himself sitting in a dungeon, locked in forever — and the takers will have the key! Forget it, baby! There ain't no causes — there ain't nothing but taking in this world and he who takes most is the smartest — and it don't make a damn bit of difference *how.*

MAMA. You making something inside me cry, son. Some awful pain inside me.

RUTH. (*crosses* R. *to* C.) Walter —

WALTER. Don't cry, Mama. Understand. That white man is going to walk in that door able to write checks for more money than we ever had. It's important to him and I'm going to help him — I'm going to put on the show, Mama.

MAMA. (*advancing resolutely*) Son — I come from five generations of people who was slaves and share croppers — but ain't nobody in my family never took no money from nobody that was a way of telling us we wasn't fit to walk the earth. We ain't never been that poor. (*raising her eyes and looking at him*) We ain't never been that — (*Voice breaks and she turns away, unable to continue.*) — dead inside.

BENEATHA. Well — we are dead now. All that talk about dreams and sunlight that goes on in this house. It's all dead now.

WALTER. What's the matter with you all! I didn't make this world! (*RUTH crosses* L. *front of table.*) It was given to me this way! Hell yes, I want me some yachts some day! Yes, I want to hang some real pearls round my wife's neck! Ain't she supposed to wear no pearls? Somebody tell me — tell who it is decides which woman is supposed to wear pearls in this world? I tell you I am a MAN—and I think my wife should wear some pearls in this world. (*This last line hangs a good while and WALTER crosses L. front of sofa to C., the word "Man" has penetrated his own consciousness perhaps more than anyone else's and he mumbles it to himself repeatedly with strange agitated pauses between as he moves about.*)

MAMA. Baby, how you going to feel on the inside?

WALTER. Fine!—Going to feel fine—a man—

MAMA. You won't have nothing left then, Walter Lee.

WALTER. (*coming to her*) I'm going to feel fine, Mama. I'm going to look that son-of-a-bitch in the eyes and say—(*He falters but presses on—punishing himself, whipping himself and his mother.*) that's *your* neighborhood out there! You got the right to keep it like you want! You got the right to have it like you want! Just write the check and—the house is yours. And—and I am going to say—(*His voice almost breaks.*) and you—you people just put the money in my hand and you won't have to live next to this bunch of STINKING NIGGERS! (*as the others react:*) Maybe—maybe I'll just get down on my black knees—(*He does so, angled half out toward the audience, but still playing to MAMA, as she, RUTH and BENEATHA watch in frozen horror.*) "Captain, Mistuh, Bossman—" (*grovelling and grinning, rolling his eyes and ringing his hands in imitation of the slow-witted movie stereotype*) "Ah-hee-hee-hee! O, yasssuh, boss! Yasssuh, Great White—" (*His voice breaks, he forces himself to go on.*) "—Father! (*He grabs his hat, hollows it and holds it out begging*) Just gi' ussen de money fo' God's sake and we's—we's ain't gwine out deh 'n' dirty up yo' white folks' neighborhood—" (*It hangs. He turns to MAMA.*) And I'll feel fine! Fine! FINE! (*He rises and, summoning his last resources, walks into his room.*)

BENEATHA. That is not a man. That is nothing but a toothless rat.

(*RUTH remains far* L. *in kitchen.*)

MAMA. Yes—death done come in this here house. (*She is nodding, slowly, reflectively.*) Done come walking in my house. On the lips of my children. You what supposed to be my beginning again. You—what supposed to be my harvest. How did we get to this here place? (*to BENEATHA*) You mournin' your brother?

BENEATHA. He's no brother of mine. (*rises, crosses to* C.)

MAMA. What you say?

BENEATHA. (*halts* L. *of sofa*) I said that that individual in that room is no brother of mine.

MAMA. That's what I thought you said. You feeling like you better than he is today? (*BENEATHA does not answer. Rising and crossing towards her*) Yeah? What you tell him a minute ago? That he wasn't a man? Yeah? You give him up for me? You done wrote his epitaph, too—like the rest of the world? Who give you that privilege?

BENEATHA. (*crosses* D.C. *above the coffee table*) Will you be on my side for once! You saw what he just did, Mama! You saw him—down on his knees. Wasn't it you who taught me to despise any man who would do that? Do what he's going to do?

MAMA. Yes—I taught you that. Me and your daddy. But I thought I taught you something else, too—I thought I taught you to love him.

BENEATHA. Love him? There is nothing left to love.

MAMA. (*answering herself as well*) There is always something left to love. And if you ain't learned that you ain't learned nothing. (*looking at her*) Have you cried for that boy today? I don't mean for yourself and for the family 'cause we lost the money. I mean for him; what he been through and what it done to him. Child, when do you think is the time to love somebody the most—when they done good and made things easy for everybody? Well, that ain't the time at all. It's when he's at his lowest and can't believe in hisself 'cause the world done whipped him so...When you starts measuring somebody—measure him right, child. Measure him right. Make sure you done taken into account what hills and valleys he come through before he got to wherever he is. (*She sighs and sits in armchair.*)

TRAVIS. (*He bursts into the room at the end of the speech, leaving the door open. Crosses* D.C. *to* L. *end of sofa.*) Grandmama—the moving men are downstairs! The truck just pulled up.

MAMA. (*turning away to conceal her agitation*) Are they, baby? They downstairs?

(*LINDNER appears in the doorway. He peers in and knocks lightly, superficially, to gain attention, and comes in. All turn to look at him.*)

LINDNER. (*brief case in hand*) Uh—hello—

(*RUTH, the closest to him, turns her back. He removes his hat. She crosses* R. *to bedroom mechanically and opens the door and lets it swing open freely and slowly as the lights come up on WALTER within, sitting at the far corner of the room. He looks out through the room to LINDNER.*)

RUTH. He's here.

(*A long minute passes and WALTER slowly gets up.*)

LINDNER. (*heartily*) Well, I certainly was glad to hear from you people. (*He smiles at BENEATHA — who turns away, rising from the coffee table and crossing extreme* L. *to kitchen sink. He ignores this and crosses to* L. *end of table with efficiency, putting his briefcase on the table. Amiably:*) Life can really be so much simpler than people let it be most of the time. (*He sits and takes out the contract and a fountain pen. WALTER has begun the trek across his room, slowly, awkwardly — rather like a small boy, passing the back of his sleeve from time to time across his mouth. As he stands in the door at last, LINDNER unscrews his pen.*) Well — with whom do I negotiate — you, Mrs. Younger, or your son here? (*There is no response from MAMA who sits with her hands folded on her lap and her eyes closed. TRAVIS, curious, goes up close to LINDNER and looks expectantly at the papers.*) Just some official papers, sonny.

RUTH. (*sharply, crossing* D.R. *of sofa*) Travis, you go downstairs —

MAMA. (*opening her eyes and looking into WALTER's*) No! Travis — you stay right here! (*She motions to TRAVIS who crosses to her.*) And you make him understand what you doing, Walter Lee. You teach him good. Like Willy Harris taught you. (*WALTER looks from her to the boy, who grins at him merrily, but she is implacable.*) You show where our five generations done come to. Go ahead, son. (*WALTER takes a step towards her, but she folds her hands and closes her eyes.*) Go ahead.

(*WALTER crosses to LINDNER, who is immersed in a final review of the contract.*)

NER, who is immersed in a final review of the contract.)

WALTER. Well, Mr. Lindner. (*LINDNER looks up and smiles and BENEATHA turns her back on the scene.*) We called you—(*There is a profound simple groping quality in his speech.*) because, well, me and my family—(*He looks about, shifting from foot to foot.*) well—we are very plain people—

LINDNER. Well, yes, Mr. Younger...

WALTER. I mean—I have worked as a chauffeur most of my life—and my wife here, she does domestic work in people's kitchens. So does my mother. I mean—we are plain people.

LINDNER. (*turns his attention to the contract*) Yes, I see, Mr. Younger....

WALTER. (*looking at his father's picture and then at the man*) And—uh—well, my father, well—he was a laborer most of his life—

LINDNER. (*turning a page, only half listening, impatient to get on with it and just a little more patronizing than he means to be*) Yes, yes, I understand....

WALTER. (*a beat; staring at him*) And my father—(*with sudden intensity as the anger rises in him at the man's indifference and his own humiliation*) My father almost *beat a man to death once* because this man called him a bad name or something. (*evenly—he is taut with emotion but not shouting.*) *You know what I mean?*

LINDNER. (*looking up, frozen*) No, no, I'm afraid I don't—(*The tension crackles.*)

WALTER. Yeah. Well—(*relaxing a little as he deliberately steps back from the precipice.*) what I mean to say is that we come from people who had a lot of pride. I mean—we are very proud people. (*MAMA has her eyes closed and is rocking back and forth as though she were in church with her head nodding the amen yes. LINDNER is paying strict attention now, but WALTER no longer cares. He has found himself and it is as if the other barely exists.)* And that's my sister over there—and she's going to be a doctor. And we are very proud.

(BENEATHA turns slowly to face him.)

LINDNER. *(utterly confused)* Well—I am sure that is very nice, but—

WALTER. What I am telling you is that we called you over here to tell you that we are very proud and that this—*(signalling to TRAVIS)* Travis, come here. *(TRAVIS crosses, grins at him, and WALTER draws him before him.)* This is my son and he makes the sixth generation of our family in this country—and we have *all* thought about your offer—

LINDNER. *(holding out the pen, anxious to get the signature and get out)* Well, good . . . good—

WALTER. And we have decided to move into our house—because my father—my father—he earned it for us, brick by brick. *(BENEATHA crosses jubilantly to MAMA, who takes her daughter's hand and begins to pat it.)* We don't want to make no trouble for nobody or fight no causes—and we will try to be good neighbors. And that's *all* we got to say about that. *(This is not an apology but a simple statement of fact—and implicitly a warning. In effect: "It's your move now. This was our last overture. From now on expect from us what we get from you." He looks the man absolutely in the eyes to be sure he is understood.)* We don't want your money.

LINDNER. *(disbelievingly, looking around at all of them)* I take it then—that you have decided to occupy!?

BENEATHA. That's what the *man* said.

LINDNER. (*to MAMA in her reverie: crossing to her*) Then I would like to appeal to you, Mrs. Younger. You are older and wiser—

MAMA. (*with an abrupt wave of the hand*) I am afraid you don't understand. My son said we was going to move and there ain't nothin' left for me to say. (*briskly*) You know how these young folks is nowadays, Mister. Can't do a thing with 'em!

LINDNER. But—

MAMA. (*rises.*) Goodbye!

LINDNER. (*folding up his materials*) Well—if you are that final about it. There is nothing left for me to say. (*He finishes almost ignored by the family, who are concentrating on WALTER LEE. At the door he halts and looks around.*) I sure hope you people know what you're getting into. (*He shakes his head and exits.*)

RUTH. (*looking around and coming to life*) Well for God's sake—if the moving men are here—(*It is a shout of joy echoed by another from BENEATHA.*) LET'S GET THE HELL OUT OF HERE!

MAMA. (*rises, crosses* L. *to kitchen*) Ain't it the truth. Look at all this here mess. Ruth, put Travis' good jacket on him—Walter Lee, fix your tie and tuck your shirt in —you look just like somebody's hoodlum. Lord, have mercy, where is my plant? (*She flies* L. *to kitchen window to get it amongst general bustling among the family, which is deliberately trying to ignore the nobility of the past moment. RUTH and WALTER find each other and embrace for a long moment.*) Y'all start on down— Travis, child, don't go empty-handed—Ruth, where did I put that box with my skillets? I'm going to make us the biggest dinner we ever ate tonight—Beneatha, what's the matter with them stockings? Pull them things up, girl—

(*The family starts to file out as moving men appear and start carrying out the heavier pieces.*)

BENEATHA. Mama, Asagai — asked me to marry him and go to Africa —

MAMA. (*in the middle of her getting-ready activity*) He did? You ain't old enough to marry nobody — (*seeing one moving man lifting one of her chairs precariously*) Darling, that ain't no bale of cotton; I got to sit in it again! I had that chair twenty-five years — (*MOVING MAN, frozen in mid-motion, gives her a look, lowers it gingerly to chest-level, turns and, like a ballet dancer balancing nitro-glycerin through a minefield, carries it out.*)

BENEATHA. (*girlishly and unreasonably trying to pursue the conversation*) To go to Africa, Mama — be a doctor in Africa —

MAMA. (*distracted*) Yes, baby —

WALTER. Africa! What he want you to go to Africa for?

BENEATHA. To practice there —

WALTER. Girl, if you don't get all them silly ideas out your head. You better marry yourself a man with some loot —

BENEATHA. (*angrily, precisely as in the first scene of the play*) What have you got to do with who I marry!

WALTER. Plenty. Now I think George Murchison —

(*He and BENEATHA go out yelling at one another vigorously — and the anger is loud and real as their voices diminish.*)

BENEATHA. (*offstage*) George Murchison! I wouldn't marry him if he was Adam and I was Eve!

(*RUTH stands at the door and turns to MAMA and smiles knowingly.*)

MAMA. (*fixing her hat at last*) Yeah — they something, all right, my children.

RUTH. Yeah — they're something. Let's go, Lena.

MAMA. (*stalling, starting to look around at the house*) Yes — I'm coming. Ruth —

RUTH. Yes?

MAMA. (*quietly, woman to woman*) He finally come to manhood today, didn't he? Kind of like a rainbow after the rain —

RUTH. (*biting her lip lest her own pride explode in front of MAMA*) Yes, Lena.

WALTER. (O.S. *calling raucously*) Y'all come on now. These people charges by the hour you know!

MAMA. (*waving RUTH out vaguely*) All right, honey — go on down   I be down directly.

(*RUTH hesitates, then exits. MAMA stands at last, alone in the living room, her plant on the table before her as the lights start to come down. For a long, long moment, she looks around and up and out at all the walls and ceilings, crosses* U.R. *to what was once her and Big Walter's bedroom, touches the door jam, crosses* C. *and suddenly, despite her, a great heaving thing rises in her and she puts her fist to her mouth to stifle it, takes a final desperate look, pulls her coat about her, pats her hat and exits.—The lights come down even more—and she comes back in, grabs her plant, and goes out for the last time. Lights down and out.*)

FINAL CURTAIN

This sequence, originally part of Act Two,
Scene 2, begins with Beneatha's exit on p. 86.

(*She exits quickly and MAMA stands looking at the
place where she stood, smiling a little perhaps.
RUTH enters.*)

RUTH. Now don't you fool with any of that stuff,
Lena—
MAMA. Oh, I just thought I'd sort a few things out. Is
Brother here?
RUTH. Yes.
MAMA. (*with concern*) Is he—
RUTH. (*reading her eyes*) Yes.

(*MAMA is silent and someone knocks on the door.
MAMA and RUTH exchange weary and knowing
glances and RUTH goes to the door with displeased
resignation and opens it to admit the neighbor,
MRS. JOHNSON, who is a rather squeaky wide-
eyed lady of no particular age, with a newspaper
under her arm.*)

MAMA. (*changing her expression to acute delight and
a ringing cheerful greeting*) Oh—hello there, Johnson.
JOHNSON. (*This is a woman who decided long ago to
be enthusiastic about EVERYTHING in life and she is*

—————————————
*See pp. 6-7 of "A Note About This Edition."

inclined to wave her wrist vigorously at the height of her exclamatory comments.) Hello there, yourself! H'you this evening, Ruth?

RUTH. (*not much of a deceptive type*) Fine, Mis' Johnson, h'you?

JOHNSON. Fine. (*reaching out quickly, playfully, and patting RUTH's stomach*) Ain't you starting to poke out none yet! (*She mugs with delight at the over-familiar remark and her eyes dart around looking at the crates and packing preparation; MAMA's face is a cold sheet of endurance.*) Oh, ain't we getting ready round here, though! Yessir! Lookathere! I'm telling you the Youngers is really getting ready to "move on up a little higher!" — Bless God!

MAMA. (*a little drily, doubting the total sincerity of the Blesser*) Bless God.

JOHNSON. He's good, ain't He?

MAMA. Oh yes, He's good.

JOHNSON. I mean sometimes He works in mysterious ways . . . but He works, don't He!

MAMA. (*the same*) Yes, he does.

JOHNSON. I'm just soooooo happy for y'all. And this here child — (*about RUTH*) looks like she could just pop open with happiness, don't she. Where's all the rest of the family?

MAMA. Bennie's gone to bed —

JOHNSON. Ain't no . . . (*The implication is pregnancy.*) sickness done hit you — (*a beat*) — I hope. . . ?

MAMA. No — she just tired. She was out this evening.

JOHNSON. (*All is a coo, an emphatic coo.*) Aw — ain't that lovely. She still going out with the little Murchison boy?

MAMA. (*drily*) Ummmm huh.

JOHNSON. That's lovely. You sure got lovely children,

Younger. [Me and Isaiah talks all the time 'bout what fine
children you was blessed with. We sure do.]

MAMA. (*to interrupt the stream of gossip*) Ruth, give Mis'
Johnson a piece of sweet potato pie and some milk.

JOHNSON. Oh honey, I can't stay hardly a minute—
(*marches to table; MAMA sits too.*) I just dropped in to
see if there was anything I could do. (*accepting the food
easily*) I guess y'all seen the news whats all over the colored
paper this week...

MAMA. No—didn't get mine yet this week.

JOHNSON. (*lifting her head and blinking with the
spirit of catastrophe*) You mean you ain't read 'bout
them colored people that was bombed out their place
out there? (*hands MAMA paper*)

(*RUTH straightens with concern and reads it too. JOHN-
SON notices her and feeds commentary.*)

JOHNSON. Ain't it something how bad these here white
folks is getting here in Chicago! Lord, getting so you
think you right down in Mississippi! (*with a tremendous
and rather insincere sense of melodrama*) 'Course I
thinks it's wonderful how our folks keeps on pushing
out. You hear some of these Negroes round here talking
'bout how they don't go where they ain't wanted and all
that—but not me, honey! (*This is a lie.*) Wilhemenia
Othella Johnson goes anywhere, any time she feels like
it! (*with head movement for emphasis*) Yes I do! Why if
we left it up to these here crackers, the poor niggers
wouldn't have nothing—(*She clasps her hand over her
mouth.*) Oh, I always forgets you don't 'low that word
in your house.

MAMA. (*quietly, looking at her*) No—I don't 'low it.

JOHNSON. (*vigorously again*) Me neither! [I was just

telling Isaiah yesterday when he come using it in front of me—I said, "Isaiah, it's just like Mis' Younger says all the time—"]

MAMA. Don't you want some more pie?

JOHNSON. No—no thank you; this was lovely. I got to get on over home and have my midnight coffee. (*A beat. She waits to be served it. When she isn't:*) I hear some people say it don't let them sleep but I finds I can't close my eyes right lessen I done had that laaaast cup of coffee...(*She waits. A beat. Undaunted.*) My Goodnight coffee, I calls it!

MAMA. (*with much eye-rolling and communication between herself and RUTH*) Ruth, why don't you give Mis' Johnson her Goodnight coffee.

(*RUTH looks up from the paper and gives MAMA an unpleasant look for her kindness.*)

JOHNSON. (*accepting the coffee which RUTH pours without friendliness*) Where's Brother tonight?

MAMA. He's lying down.

JOHNSON. MMmmmmm, he sure gets his beauty rest, don't he? Good-looking man. Sure is a good-looking man! (*reaching out to pat RUTH's stomach again*) I guess that's how come we keep on having babies around here. (*She winks at MAMA, who dislikes her vulgarity and looks away.*) One thing 'bout Brother, he always know how to have a *good* time. And soooooo ambitious! I bet it was his idea y'all moving out to Clybourne Park. Lord—I bet this time next month y'all's names will have been in the papers plenty—(*holding up her hands to mark off each word of the headline she can see in front of her*) "NEGROES INVADE CLYBOURNE PARK--BOMBED!"

MAMA. (*She and RUTH look at the woman in amazement.*) We ain't exactly moving out there to get bombed.

JOHNSON. Oh, honey—you know I'm praying to God every day that don't nothing like that happen! But you have to think of life like it is—and these here Chicago peckerwoods is some baaaad peckerwoods.

MAMA. (*wearily*) We done thought about all that, Mis' Johnson.

(*BENEATHA comes out of the bedroom in her robe and passes through to the bathroom. MRS. JOHNSON turns.*)

JOHNSON. Hello there, Bennie!

BENEATHA. (*crisply*) Hello, Mrs. Johnson.

JOHNSON. How is school?

BENEATHA. (*crisply*) Fine, thank you. (*She goes out.*)

JOHNSON. (*insulted*) Getting so she don't have much to say to nobody.

MAMA. The child was on her way to the bathroom.

JOHNSON. I know—but sometimes she act like ain't got time to pass the time of day with nobody ain't been to college. Oh—I ain't criticizing her none.[It's just—you know how some of our young people gets when they get a little education. (*MAMA and RUTH say nothing, just look at her.*) Yes—well. Well, I guess I better get on home. (*unmoving*) 'Course] I can understand how she must be proud and everything—being the only one in the family to make something of herself! I know just being a chauffeur ain't never satisfied Brother none. He shouldn't feel like that, though. Ain't nothing wrong with being a chauffeur.

MAMA. There's plenty wrong with it.

JOHNSON. What?

MAMA. Plenty. My husband always said being any kind of a servant wasn't a fit thing for a man to have to be. He always said a man's hands was made to make things, or to turn the earth with — not to drive nobody's car for 'em — or — (*She looks at her own hands.*) carry they slop jars. And my boy is just like him — he wasn't meant to wait on nobody.

JOHNSON. (*rising, somewhat offended*) Mmmmm mmmm. The Youngers is too much for me! (*She looks around.*) You sure one proud-acting bunch of colored folks. Well—[I always thinks like Booker T. Washington said that time — "Education has spoiled many a good plow hand" —

MAMA. Is that what old Booker T. said?

JOHNSON. He sure did.

MAMA. Well, it sounds just like him. (*A beat. With flavor*) The fool.

JOHNSON. (*indignantly*) Well — he was one of our great men.

MAMA. Who said so?

JOHNSON. (*nonplussed*) You know, me and you ain't never agreed about some things, Lena Younger.] I guess I better be going—

RUTH. (*quickly*) Good night.

JOHNSON. Good night. Oh — (*thrusting it at her*) You can *keep* the paper! (*a beat; with a trill*) Nighty-night.

MAMA. Good night, Mis' Johnson.

(*MRS. JOHNSON exits.*)

RUTH. If ignorance was gold . . .

MAMA. Shush. Don't talk about folks behind their backs.

RUTH. You do.

MAMA. I'm old and corrupted. (*BENEATHA enters.*) You was rude to Mis' Johnson, Beneatha, and I don't like it at all.

BENEATHA. (*at her door*) Mama, if there are two things we, as a people, have got to overcome, one is the Ku Klux Klan—and the other is (*a beat*) Wilhemenia Othella Johnson! (*She exits.*)

MAMA. Smart aleck.

(*The phone rings.*)

RUTH. I'll get it.

MAMA. Lord, ain't this a popular place tonight.

Act Two, Scene 2 now continues with Ruth's phone conversation on p. 87.

II
This sequence follows Beneatha's line, "Yes—really," on page 46, line 10:

(*There is a sudden commotion from the street and BE-NEATHA goes to the window to look out.*)

BENEATHA. What on earth is going on out there. These kids! (*There are, as she throws open the window, the shouts of children rising up from below. She sticks her head out to see better and calls out.*) TRAVIS! TRAVIS!...WHAT ARE YOU DOING DOWN THERE? (*She sees.*) Oh, Lord, they're chasing a rat!

(*RUTH covers her face with hands and turns away.*)

MAMA. (*angrily.*) Tell that youngun to get himself up here, at once!

BENEATHA. TRAVIS...YOU COME UPSTAIRS...AT ONCE!

RUTH. (*her face twisted*) Chasing a rat...

MAMA. (*looking at RUTH, worried.*) Doctor say everything going to be all right?

RUTH. (*far away*) Yes - she says everything is going to be fine—

MAMA. (*immediately suspicious*) "She"? What doctor you went to?

(*RUTH just looks at MAMA meaningfully and MAMA opens her mouth to speak as TRAVIS bursts in.*)

TRAVIS. (*excited and full of narrative, coming directly to his mother*) Mama, you should of seen the rat...Big as a cat, honest! (*He shows an exaggerated size with his hands.*) Gaaleee, that rat was really cuttin' and Bubber caught him with his heel and the janitor, Mr. Barnett, got him with a stick —and then they got him in a corner and — BAM! BAM! BAM! — and he was still jumping round and bleeding like everything too — There's rat blood all over the street—

(*RUTH reaches out suddenly and grabs her son without even looking at him and clamps her hand over his mouth and holds him to her, as all stare at her startled. MAMA crosses to them and takes the boy from her.*)

MAMA. You hush up now...talking all that terrible stuff...

(*TRAVIS is staring at his mother with a stunned expression. BENEATHA comes quickly and takes him away from his grandmother and ushers him to the door.*)

BENEATHA. You go back outside and play...but not with any rats. (*She pushes him gently out the door with the boy straining to see what is wrong with his mother.*)

The scene now resumes on p. 46, line 17, with MAMA hovering worriedly over Ruth: "Ruth honey—what's the matter with you—you sick?"

Depending upon space limitations, you might wish to include some or all of the following in your playbill:

LORRAINE HANSBERRY ON PLAYWRIGHTING*

I am a writer. I suppose I think that the highest gift that man has is art, and I am audacious enough to think of myself as an artist — that there is both joy and beauty and illumination and communion between people to be achieved through the dissection of personality. That's what I want to do. I want to reach a little closer to the world, which is to say to people, and see if we can share some illuminations together about each other.

* * *

Hotel Taft
New Haven, Conn.
January 19, 1959

Dear Mother,

Well — here we are. I am sitting alone in a nice hotel room in New Haven, Conn. Downstairs, next door in the Shubert Theatre, technicians are putting the finishing touches on a living room that is supposed to be a Chicago living room. Wednesday the curtain goes up at 8 P.M. The next day the New Haven papers will say what they think about our efforts. A great deal of money has been spent and a lot of people have done

---

some hard, hard work, and it may be the beginning of many different careers.

The actors are very good and the director is a very talented man — so if it is a poor show I won't be able to blame a soul but your youngest daughter.

Mama, it is a play that tells the truth about people, Negroes and life and I think it will help a lot of people to understand how we are just as complicated as they are — and just as mixed up — but above all, that we have among our miserable and downtrodden ranks — people who are the very essence of human dignity. That is what, after all the laughter and tears, the play is supposed to say. I hope it will make you very proud. See you soon. Love to all,

Lorraine

* * *

I was born on the Southside of Chicago. I was born black and a female. I was born in a depression after one world war, and came into my adolescence during another. While I was still in my teens the first atom bombs were dropped on human beings at Nagasaki and Hiroshima, and by the time I was twenty-three years old my government and that of the Soviet Union had entered actively into the worst conflict of nerves in human history — the Cold War.

I have lost friends and relatives through cancer, lynching and war. I have been personally the victim of physical attack which was the offspring of racial and political hysteria. I have worked with the handicapped and seen the ravages of congenital diseases that we have not yet conquered because we spend our time and ingenuity in far less purposeful wars. I see daily on the streets of New York, street gangs and prostitutes and beggars; I know people afflicted with drug addiction and alcoholism and mental illness; I have, like all of you, on a thousand occasions seen indescribable displays of man's very real inhumanity to man; and I have come to maturity, as we all must, knowing that greed and malice, indifference to human misery and, perhaps above all else, ignorance—the prime ancient and persistent enemy of man—abound in this world.

I say all of this to say that one cannot live with sighted eyes and feeling heart and not know and react to the miseries which afflict this world.

I have given you this account so that you know that what I write is not based on the assumption of idyllic possibilities or innocent assessments of the true nature of life—but, rather, my own personal view that, posing one against the other, I think that the human race does not command its own destiny and that that destiny can eventually embrace the stars. . . .

> (From an address to a black
> writers conference, March 1, 1959)

* * *

INTERVIEWER: The question, I'm sure, is asked you many times—you may be tired of it—someone comes up to you and says: "This is not really a Negro play; why, this could be about anybody! It's a play about people!" What is your reaction? What do you say?

L. H.: Well I hadn't noticed the contradiction because I'd always been under the impression that Negroes *are* people. But actually it's an excellent question because I do know what people are trying to say. They're trying to say that it isn't a propanganda play, that it isn't something that hits you over the head; they are trying to say that they believe the characters in our play transcend category. However, it is an unfortunate way to try and say it, because I believe that one of the most sound ideas in dramatic writing is that in order to create the universal, you must pay very great attention to the specific. Universality, I think, emerges from truthful identity of what is.

In other words, I have told people that not only is this a Negro family, specifically and definitely culturally, but it's not even a New York family or a southern Negro family. It is specifically Southside Chicago . . . that kind of care, that kind of attention to detail. In other words, I think people, to the extent we accept them and believe them as who they're supposed to be, to that extent they can become everybody. So I would say it is definitely a Negro play before it is anything else. . . .

* * *

My dear Miss Oehler:

. . . Let us please be quite clear about one thing: I have treated Mr. Lindner as a human being merely because he is one; that does not make the meaning of his call less malignant, less sick. I could no more imagine myself allowing the Youngers to accept his obscene offer of money than I could imagine myself allowing them to accept a cash payment for their own murder. . . .

You see, our people don't really have a choice. We must come out of the ghettos of America, because the ghettos are killing us; not only our dreams, as Mama says, but our very bodies. It is not an abstraction to us that the average American Negro has a life expectancy of five to ten years less than the average white. You see,

Miss Oehler, that is murder, and a Negro writer cannot be expected to share the placid view of the situation that might be the case with a white writer.

As for changing "the hearts of individuals" — I am glad the American nation did not wait for the hearts of individual slave owners to change to abolish the slave system — for I suspect that I should still be running around on a plantation as a slave. And that really would not do.

Sincerely,

* * *

INTERVIEWER: Are you trying to find tragedy in these people? In the smaller people?

L. H.: Ultimately I would like to, yes — it's the route that I'm trying to go.

INTERVIEWER: That's fascinating. Would you call your plays naturalistic?

L. H.: I would not.

INTERVIEWER: And what would you call them? If you had to put it in words.

L. H.: I hope that my work is genuine realism.

INTERVIEWER: What's the difference?

L. H.: It's enormously different. Well, naturalism tends to take the world as it is and say: this is what it is, this is how it happens, it is "true" because we see it every day in life that way — you know, you simply photograph the garbage can. But in realism — I think the artist who is creating the realistic work imposes on it not only what *is* but what is *possible* . . . because that is part of reality too. So that you get a much larger potential of what

man can do. And it requires a much greater selectivity — you don't just put everything that *seems* — you put what you believe is. . . .

* * *

Nov. 27, 1961

In life, adequate respect must be paid to the tenacity of the absurd in both human and natural affairs. That drama which will ignore the effect and occasional domination of the absurd on the designs of the will of men will lack an ultimate stature, I think. But similarly, attention must be paid in equal and careful measure to the frequent triumph of man, if not nature, *over* the absurd.

Perhaps it is here that certain of the modern existentialists have erred. They have seemed to me to be overwhelmed by the mere fact of the absurd and become incapable of imagining *its* frailty. (The balance which is struck between the recognition of both — man's defeat *and* triumph in the face of absurdity — may be the final secret of Shakespeare). . . .

* * *

[Undated] —

If anything should happen — before 'tis done — may I trust that all commas and periods will be placed and someone will complete my thoughts —

This last should be the least difficult — since there are so many who think as I do —

Coffee
Eggs (2 each performance)
Toast (2 pieces each performance)
Instant oatmeal
Butter
Bottle of milk
Box of crackers
Beer (3 bottles each performance)
Sugar
Salt, Pepper
(Bread bag w/slices)

Coffee pot
3 iron skillets
2 saucepans
2 pot holders
6 each—knives, forks, spoons
Sugar bowl
Salt and pepper shakers
Mixing bowl
3 bowls
Sewing basket and accessories
School books with strap
2 textbooks
1 looseleaf book
1 telephone
1 laundry basket (filled)
Electric iron
Ironing board (no legs)
Laundry sprinkler
Dummy foods for refrigerator

Chicago Tribune
2 kitchen aprons
6 each—plates, cups, saucers
4 face towels
2 kitchen towels, holder
2 sink sponges
1 can cleanser
Cut glass fruit bowl
6 pieces of wax fruit
Lace tablecloth
Plastic tablecloth
Alarm clock
2 toothbrushes
Plastic drinking glass
(1 each performance)
Soap in case
Tube of toothpaste
Old corn broom
New corn broom
Mop and pail
Carpet sweeper
Can furniture wax
Dust rag
Old newspapers
Low vase with artificial flowers
Woman's handbag with:
1 change purse
Coins
Pocket comb
Cigarettes
Lipstick
Matches
$1.00 bill

Woman's hairbrush
Plant in pot
Beer can opener
2 Ash trays
Three shirts on hangers
2 records in jackets
Envelope of money
2 string shopping bags with groceries
1 large wooden crate
1 old-fashioned trunk
1 small step unit
1 barrel
3 cardboard cartons
2 suitcases (old)
Pair of window curtains in bag
Calling cards (1 each performance)
2 blankets
2 pillows
2 sheets
Legal forms (1 each performance)
Punch card check (1 each performance)
Typed list (1 each performance)
Mailing envelopes
Toaster
Dustpan
Breakable glass (1 each performance)
Shoulder bag w/lipstick
Mug (Mama's)
Pictures on walls
2 throw pillows
Rug under sofa

Cardboard box with:
Ribbon
Tissue paper
Envelope w/card
Hand trowel
Hand cultivator
Hand rake
Cardboard box with:
Ribbon
Nigerian costume
Phono record in jacket
Boy's toys
Broomstick
Rubber ball
Plastic waste basket
6 pair of socks
Kitchen matches
2 camera cases
Guitar case
Insect spray gun
Grease pencil
Sticks and string for plant
Hat box
Gardening hat (large)
Zippered brief case with legal papers, pens
Covered butter dish
Sock egg
Slip of paper with address
Paperbag with ball of cord
2 maracas
Curtains on window
Windowshade
Doilies (armchair, sofa)
Stereo
3 Ebony magazines
Standing lamp by armchair
Calendar on front door

Hot pads (stove, table)
Notes and recipes (on refrigerator)
Lamp w/shade (buffet)
Lamp w/shade (bedr. bureau)

Shaving kit
Standing pictures (buffet, bureau)
Mirror (inner closet door)
Matches (Walter's pockets)

COSTUME PLOT

RUTH

Act One, Scene 1
Nightgown, Robe
Slippers, Hairclips
During scene add:
Half-apron

Act One, Scene 2
Suit, Blouse
Heels, Gloves
Hat, Handbag
Light coat
Full slip, Hose
Earrings

Act Two, Scene 1
Linen dress
Half-apron (same as 1:1)
Flat shoes
(Repeat hose, slip, earrings)

Act Two, Scene 2
"Shirt" dress
Petticoat
(Repeat apron, flats, hose, earrings)

Act Two, Scene 3
Dress (more attractive per her spirits)
Heels, Half-apron,
(Repeat hose, slip, earrings)

Act Three
Same as 2:2
During scene add:
Coat, bag (same as 1:2

Permanent jewelry:
Wedding ring, watch

BENEATHA

Act One, Scene 1
Red flannel nightgown
Hair curlers
Knee pads, Scuffs
In "bathroom" lose knee pads and underdress White blouse w/Peter Pan collar, Locket
In "bedroom" change into:
Pleated skirt
Cardigan, Loafers
Black knee socks
During rest of scene add:
Coat w/hood, Scarf

Act One, Scene 2
Jeans

Man's shirt, tied at
   waist
Scarf (as face mask)
(Repeat knee socks, loafers,
   locket)
During scene add Raincoat

Act Two, Scene 1
   African robes
   Matching Headwrap
In "bedroom," change into:
   Dress w/jacket
   Heels, Hose, Purse
   Evening coat
   Pearls, Earrings

Act Two, Scene 2
   Evening dress
   Petticoat
(Repeat heels, locket, hose
coat, purse, earrings)

Act Two, Scene 3
   Cardigan
   Blouse
(Repeat pleated skirt,
   knee socks, loafers,
   locket)

Act Three
   Same as 2:3
During scene add raincoat
(same as 1:2)

*In Scenes 1:2, 2:2, 2:3
and Act 3 wear gold
"twist-o-flex"* Timex

MAMA

Act One, Scene 1
   Housedress, Hose
   Half-apron
   Black lace-up shoes
   Simple gold earrings

Act One, Scene 2
   Print housedress
   Full apron, Headwrap
(Repeat shoes, hose)

Act Two, Scene 1
   Light coat, Hat
   Suit, Black handbag
   Heels, Gloves, Hose
   Earrings
   Pearl & gold necklace

Act Two, Scene 2
   Print dress, Slip
   Hat
(Same shoes, earrings 1:1;
   coat, handbag, hose 2:1)

Act Two, Scene 3
   Dressier dress
(Repeat coat, hat, necklace,
   hose, slip, earrings as 2:1)

Act Three
   Same as 2:3

Permanent Jewelry:
   Wedding ring

WALTER LEE

Act One, Scene 1
Stocking cap
Mismatched pajamas
White T-shirt
In "bathroom," change into: *TRAVIS*
Black pants, White shirt,
Black tie, Black belt,
Black socks
On stage add:
Black chauffeur jacket
Black chauffeur cap
Black zip boots

Act One, Scene 2
Golf shirt, Slacks
Shoes, Belt, Socks
During scene add:
Windbreaker, Hat

Act Two, Scene 1
Same as 1:2

Act Two, Scene 2
(Repeat slacks, shirt,
belt, boots, tie, socks
as 1:1; hat 1:2)

Act Two, Scene 3
Cardigan
Striped tie
(Repeat slacks, shoes, belt,
socks, hat 1:2; shirt 1:1)

Act Three
Same as 2:3

TRAVIS

Permanent jewelry:
Wedding ring, Watch

Act One, Scene 1
Pajamas, Slippers
In "bathroom," change into:
Pants, White shirt,
Sweater vest, T-shirt
Socks, Shoes
Cloth belt
On stage add:
Bomber jacket
Baseball cap

Act One, Scene 2
Jeans w/rolled cuffs
Plaid flannel shirt
Black belt
(Repeat socks, cap)

Act Two, Scene 1
Same as 2:1

Act Two, Scene 2
(Repeat pajamas, slip-
pers 1:1)

Act Two, Scene 3
Pants, Tie, Belt
"Ski" sweater vest
(Repeat shirt, shoes,
socks 1:1)

During scene add and lose
Cardigan and add:
Tweed jacket

Act Three

Same as 2:3
During scene add:
   Corduroy blazer

ASAGAI

Act One, Scene 2
   3-piece black suit
   Black shoes & socks
   White shirt & T-shirt
   Tie, White suspenders

Act Three
   Sweater, Tie
   Brown sandals
(Repeat shirt, pants, socks,
   suspenders from 1:2)

GEORGE

Act Two, Scene 1
   Pleated pants, Belt
   White Shirt & T-shirt
   White bucks
   Paisly tie
   Sweater vest
   Watch, Fraternity pin

Act Two, Scene 2
   3-piece pinstriped suit
   Striped tie, Loafers
   Black sock & Belt

   Pocket square
(Repeat T-shirt, shirt,
   watch, fraternity pin)

LINDNER

Act Two, Scene 3
   3-piece brown suit
   White shirt & T-shirt
   Hat, Patterned tie
   Brown shoes & Socks
   Beige suspenders

Act Three
   Same as 2:3

BOBO

Act Two, Scene 3
   Worn suit, Patterned tie
   Brown shoes, Black socks
   Short-sleeved shirt
   Suspenders
   Felt hat, White T-shirt

MOVING MEN

Act Three
   2 green coveralls
   T-shirts
   Heavy socks
   Workboots
   1 cap

Oh Lord, I Don't Feel Noways Tired

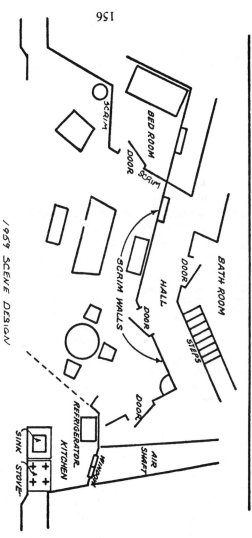

1959 SCENE DESIGN

"A RAISIN IN THE SUN"

ABOUT LORRAINE HANSBERRY

(continued from inside front cover)

In 1956, Lorraine Hansberry sat down to write a play which, as she later wrote to her mother, "tells the truth about people, Negroes and life." The play, *A Raisin in the Sun*, opened in March 1959—and, as *The New York Times* summarized on its 25th anniversary, it "changed American theatre forever." This was not just because Hansberry, the first black woman produced on Broadway, became, at 29, the youngest American, the fifth woman, and the only black dramatist ever to win the Best Play of the Year Award of the New York Drama Critics. *A Raisin in the Sun* marked a turning point because, as James Baldwin has written, "Never before in the entire history of the American theatre had so much of the truth of Black people's lives been seen on the stage."

The play had its origins in the playwright's own childhood experiences in 1930's Chicago where, in defiance of the "restrictive covenants" that confined blacks to the ghetto, her family moved into a hostile white neighborhood. Mobs surrounded the house and a huge chunk of concrete hurled through the window nearly struck the eight-year-old future author. She remembered, too, the faces of the people who "cursed and spat at and pummeled" her on the way to and from school, and the sight of her mother patrolling their home nights with a gun. The family was evicted by the Illinois courts, but her father and NAACP lawyers fought the case all the way to an historic Supreme Court decision outlawing the covenant (Hansberry vs. Lee). Despite this "victory," however, as she later wrote, "the cost, in emotional turmoil—which led to my father's early death as a permanently embittered exile in a foreign country when he saw that after such sacrificial efforts the Negroes of Chicago were as ghetto-locked as

ABOUT LORRAINE HANSBERRY

ever"—stayed with her. In *A Raisin in the Sun* she created a ghetto family poised at the final curtain, in all their complexities and contradictions though strengthened within, at the edge of a similar move into uncertainty.

In 1961, Hansberry's film adaptation of the play was nominated for Best Screenplay and won a Cannes Film Festival Award.

Published and produced in some thirty languages abroad and in thousands of productions across the U.S., *A Raisin in the Sun* was to become an American classic—"one of a handful of great American dramas . . . in the inner circle, along with *Death of a Salesman, Long Day's Journey into Night,* and *The Glass Menagerie"* *(Washington Post).* It brought into the theatre a new black audience, encouraged a new generation of black artists, playwrights, and performers. In its now legendary first cast and director, every one of whom was to make his/her own subsequent mark on theatre and film—Lloyd Richards, Sidney Poitier, Claudia McNeil, Ruby Dee, Diana Sands, Louis Gossett, Ivan Dixon, Glynn Turman, Douglas Turner Ward and Lonne Elder III—it proclaimed unmistakably the resources and depths of black talent. And perhaps most important, *A Raisin in the Sun* portended, on many levels, the revolution in consciousness that was to come: the uncompromising assertion of Afro-American identity, heritage, beauty, the inseparability of the struggle in America from that in Africa, the theme of women's liberation, and the relation of all of these to human liberation. Of 60 leading figures interviewed for a 1979 documentary film history of black theatre, producer Woodie King Jr. has summarized: "Over 40 said they had been influenced . . . by Lorraine Hansberry and her work. . . To mention all of the artists whose careers were enhanced by

ABOUT LORRAINE HANSBERRY

Hansberry would read like a 'Who's Who' in the black theatre."

Five years later, on January 12, 1965, during the run of her second play, *The Sign in Sidney Brustein's Window*, Lorraine Hansberry died of cancer. She was 34. In her short life she had participated, both as activist and artist, in some of the most momentous events of her time. In her plays she illuminated the lives and aspirations of ordinary people confronting, in their own ways, the fundamental challenges and choices of the age. "Her commitment of spirit . . . her creative literary ability and her profound grasp of the deep social issues confronting the world today," said Martin Luther King Jr. on her death, "will remain an inspiration to generations yet unborn."

These words have proved prophetic. *To Be Young, Gifted and Black*, a portrait of Hansberry in her own words, was the longest-running off-Broadway drama of 1969; it has been staged in every state of the Union, recorded, filmed, televised, turned into a popular song by Nina Simone, and the title phrase itself (from her last speech) has entered the language in countless permutations. *Les Blancs* (The Whites), her drama of black/white confrontation in revolutionary Africa, was presented posthumously on Broadway and received the votes of six critics for the Best American Play of 1970. In 1974, the musical *Raisin*, based on *A Raisin in the Sun*, won the Tony Award as Broadway's Best Musical. Hansberry's published works include *To Be Young, Gifted and Black*, a full-length informal autobiography (not to be confused with the play), *A Raisin in the Sun and The Sign in Sidney Brustein's Window* (a New American Library double-edition), *The Movement: Documentary of a Struggle for Equality* (a

159

ABOUT LORRAINE HANSBERRY

photohistory of the civil rights struggle written for the Student Nonviolent Coordinating Committee), and *Lorraine Hansberry: The Collected Last Plays* (Plume Books, New American Library). Highlights from her speeches and interviews can be heard on the Caedmon recording *Lorraine Hansberry Speaks Out: Art and The Black Revolution*. In 1979, *Lorraine Hansberry: Art of Thunder, Vision of Light*, a retrospective assessment by leading writers, critics and playwrights, was published by the quarterly *Freedomways*. The unabridged *A Raisin in the Sun*, presented on television by American Playhouse in 1989, is available on videocassette.

LORRAINE HANSBERRY ARCHIVES

For the historic record and use by future scholars, the Hansberry Archives would be grateful to receive programs, reviews, and any other relevant materials concerning productions of the Hansberry plays. Please address these to Robert Nemiroff; P.O. Box 393; Croton-on-Hudson, N.Y. 10520.
